Mongolia

Mongolia

BY RUTH BJORKLUND

Enchantment of the World™
Second Series

CHILDREN'S PRESS®

An Imprint of Scholastic Inc.

Frontispiece: **Mongolian armed forces honorary guard**

Consultant: Morris Rossabi, PhD, Distinguished Professor of History, City University of New York
Please note: All statistics are as up-to-date as possible at the time of publication.

Book production by The Design Lab

Library of Congress Cataloging-in-Publication Data
Names: Bjorklund, Ruth, author.
Title: Mongolia / by Ruth Bjorklund.
Description: New York : Children's Press, an Imprint of Scholastic Inc., 2016. |
   Series: Enchantment of the world | Includes bibliographical references and index.
Identifiers: LCCN 2015043526 | ISBN 9780531218846 (library binding : alk. paper)
Subjects: LCSH: Mongolia—Juvenile literature.
Classification: LCC DS798 .B54 2016 | DDC 951.7/3—dc23
LC record available at http://lccn.loc.gov/2015043526

1 2 3 4 5 6 7 8 9 10 R 26 25 24 23 22 21 20 19 18 17

Mongolian wearing traditional Kazakh clothing

Contents

Left to right: **Larch trees, falconry, children playing, reindeer herders, Kazakh herder**

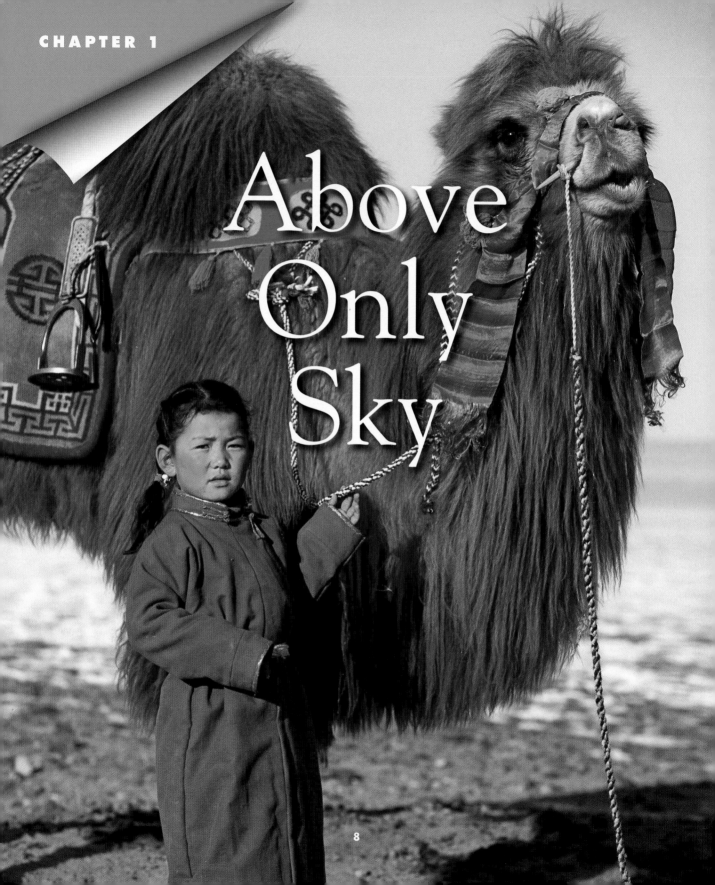

CHAPTER 1

Above Only Sky

SUREN IS FROM A SMALL VILLAGE IN MONGOLIA, a country in central Asia. For centuries, his family members have been nomadic herders who raised livestock on the steppe, a vast grassland near the Gobi Desert. They moved their animals around to find sources of fresh water and good grazing grounds. Mongolian nomads live in large, round tents called *gers*, which they pack up and take with them when they move to the next pasture. The Mongolian steppe and parts of the Gobi are well suited for herding sheep, goats, horses, yaks, and Bactrian camels. Suren's family herded camels.

Opposite: **In winter, Bactrian camels have long, woolly coats. These coats shed quickly, in large pieces, when the weather begins to warm.**

On the Steppe

Suren was proud of his family's camel herd. A Bactrian camel has two humps. It can carry 450 pounds (200 kilograms) of cargo and walk 3 to 4 miles per hour (5 to 6 kilometers per hour). Suren loves how they plod along in their odd, loping

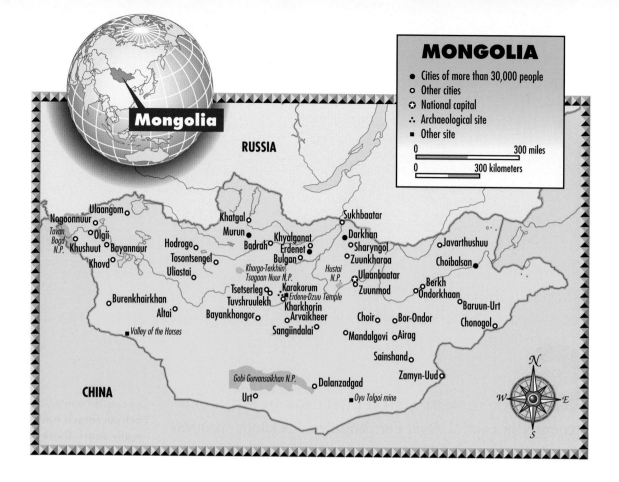

MONGOLIA

- Cities of more than 30,000 people
- Other cities
- ★ National capital
- ∴ Archaeological site
- ■ Other site

0   300 miles

0   300 kilometers

RUSSIA

CHINA

Mongolia

Ulaangom
Nogoonnuur
Tavan Bogd N.P.
Olgii
Khushuut
Bayannuur
Khovd
Hodrogo
Tosontsengel
Uliastai
Khatgal
Murun
Badrah
Khyalganat
Erdenet
Bulgan
Khorgo-Terkhiin Tsagaan Nuur N.P.
Sukhbaatar
Darkhan
Sharyngol
Zuunkharaa
Javarthushuu
Choibalsan
Hustai N.P.
Ulaanbaatar
Zuunmod
Berkh
Ondorkhaan
Baruun-Urt
Tsetserleg
Karakorum
Erdene-Dzuu Temple
Kharkhorin
Tuvshruulekh
Burenkhairkhan
Altai
Bayankhongor
Arvaikheer
Sangiindalai
Choir
Bor-Ondor
Mandalgovi
Airag
Chonogol
Valley of the Horses
Sainshand
Zamyn-Uud
Gobi Gurvansaikhan N.P.
Dalanzadgad
Urt
Oyu Tolgoi mine

N
W   E
S

way. But camels can run, too. After Suren's family settled in a new camp and unloaded the packs from the camels' backs, the camels were let loose and off they went. Some camels can outrun a horse. Camels provided Suren's family with milk and wool. Some herders also use the camels for meat, but Suren's father did not slaughter his livestock.

When Suren's family reached a new pasture, they set up their ger camp and looked for water for the camels. The region has few streams or ponds so they took water from wells. Suren was six when he began helping pull buckets of water up for the camels. A camel can drink 25 to 30 gallons (95 to 115 liters) at a time, so it takes a long time to water the herd.

Suren spent part of the year back in his village so he could attend school. He would rather have been on the steppe, but his older sister, Khulan, liked living in town. She would prefer to live in Ulaanbaatar, Mongolia's capital, where nearly half the country's population lives.

Hard Times

Then, one winter, Suren's life completely changed. The desert, steppe, and mountains experienced a brutal winter called a *zud*. Bitter cold, snow, and winds devastated the herds, and millions of animals died. Hundreds of thousands of herding

A herder drives sheep across the frozen land in western Mongolia.

families lost everything. Some people kept what few camels had survived and decided to try making a living as tour guides. In that business, tour companies send tourists to the village and the herders lead them on camel rides through the desert and steppe. The tourists stay overnight with people at "home-stays"—lodgings in the nomads' gers. The tourists enjoy the hospitality, and the income is good for the local people who have lost their traditional livelihood.

Suren's family lost their livelihood. Most of their camel herd died in the zud, and his father decided enough was enough. He gave the surviving camels to his brother, and the family packed their ger and moved to Ulaanbaatar.

In the City

The family moved to a *khasha*, one of many fenced camps of gers outside of Ulaanbaatar. Khulan excitedly made plans to spend her last year of high school in the big city and then go to the university. Suren's mother found work in a shop selling clothes and handicrafts. She had been the finest seamstress in the village, using needles that had been passed down from her grandmother. Suren's father is considering going to work in a mine in the Gobi. Suren, Khulan, and their mother do not want him to go, but mining jobs pay well.

Khulan would like their family to make enough money that they can move out of the ger and into an apartment with indoor plumbing and electric heat. Suren and his mother do not want to leave the khasha community. Their ger is home. Suren's mother says they have all they need. The ger is roomy, beauti-

ful, and comfortable, with red and blue camel-hair carpets and embroidered blankets on the walls. A cook stove in the center keeps them all warm and well fed. In Suren's sleeping area, he hangs pouches made of animal hide and felt that hold his favorite belongings, including books, a chessboard, and *shagai*, sheep anklebones he uses to play many different games.

Suren is thinking about his future, but it is uncertain. Will he go to university? Will he work in the mines? Or will he return to the steppe and build a new herd? For the time being, he will remain with his family in their ger outside the big, bustling city that is the nation's capital.

CHAPTER 2

Land of Blue Sky

MONGOLIA IS A LAND OF SPECTACULAR AND
nearly untouched beauty. Mountains, some snowcapped,
tower over a vast landscape of valleys, meadows, forests,
steppe grasslands, and deserts of ever-swirling sands. Above all
the diversity of landforms, the sun shines in a vivid blue sky.

Mongolia is the fourth-largest country on the Asian con-
tinent, more than twice the size of the U.S. state of Texas. It
is located in the eastern part of the Central Asian Plateau,
bordered by Russia to the north and China to the south.
Mongolia is completely landlocked. The nearest body of water
is the Yellow Sea in the Pacific Ocean, 435 miles (700 km) to
the east across northeast China.

Mountains

Mongolia has three major mountain ranges. In the west, the
soaring Altai Range stretches about 250 miles (400 km) from
the far west toward the south. This range includes the country's highest peak, the snowcapped Mount Huiten, which

Opposite: **Lakes nestle in
craggy valleys high in
the Altai Mountains of
western Mongolia.**

Ancient Land

More than two hundred million years ago, a vast inland sea covered much of what is now Mongolia. Over time, large chunks of the earth's outer layer, known as tectonic plates, collided, pushing up the land of Mongolia so much that it is now one of the highest countries in the world. The average elevation in Mongolia is 5,184 feet (1,580 m), or nearly 1 mile (1.6 km). Fifty million years ago, tectonic plates under the Indian subcontinent pushed Asia violently against the immovable bedrock of Siberia in what is now northeastern Russia. The force created the nearby massive mountain ranges of the Himalayas and the Pamirs. These earth movements created a "wrinkled" landscape in western Mongolia. Many fault lines, or fractures in the land, are visible today and are evidence of these ancient geologic events. A sudden movement of the rock along a fault is an earthquake. Today, Mongolia remains one of the most earthquake-prone areas in the world.

rises to 14,350 feet (4,374 meters). The Altai Range becomes the Altai-Gobi Range and extends deep into the heart of the Gobi Desert. Ikh Bogd, a striking peak standing sentinel over the Gobi, rises 12,982 feet (3,957 m).

Mongolia's oldest mountains are the gently rounded Khentii Mountains, which run from the capital of Ulaanbaatar northeast toward Russia. Burkhan Khaldun, the most prominent mountain of the range, is sacred to the Mongolian people because it is considered the birthplace of the Mongolian nation.

The Khangai Mountains are in the western part of central Mongolia. The mountains, which were partially formed by volcanoes, are rounded, forested, and show the remains of many lava flows. The range's highest peak is Otgon Tenger, which rises 13,192 feet (4,021 m) and is permanently covered in ice. North of the Khangai Mountains, on the Russian border, rises the heavily forested Hovsgol range.

Tundra and Steppe

Mongolia's high mountains are covered in tundra (a treeless frozen plain), meadows, marshes, and in some cases, glaciers. Mongolia's taiga forest, located in the northern part of the

A reindeer herder makes his way through Mongolia's taiga forest.

Digging into the Past

The Flaming Cliffs are a region of red rocky outcroppings located in a heavily volcanic area of the Gobi Desert. American explorer Roy Chapman Andrews wrote of the Flaming Cliffs, "There appear to be medieval castles with spires and turrets, brick-red in the evening light, colossal gateways, walls and ramparts."

In 1922, Andrews led an expedition through the area to search for evidence of early humans, but failed to discover much new scientific information. He was ready to give up on the project for the winter. While setting up camp to wait for the rest of his exploratory team, his photographer looked down and saw an ancient fossil lying on the ground. Scientists began unearthing one of the world's most important fossil beds.

The area became a wealth of information about the Cretaceous period, which lasted from about 145 to 65 million years ago. Returning the following summer, Andrews and his team uncovered the fossilized remains of dinosaurs such as *Protoceratops*, *Velociraptor*, and the ancestors of *Tyrannosaurus rex*, along with ancient crocodiles, giant rhinoceroses, and fossilized dinosaur eggs. They also uncovered evidence of early human settlements. Today, paleontologists, people who study the fossils of plants and animals, continue to make exciting discoveries in the region.

country, is the southernmost portion of the Siberian taiga, the earth's wildest, largest, and most heavily forested region.

Mongolia's mountainous forest-steppe region occurs in the lower elevations of the major mountain ranges and covers about a quarter of the country. Forests fed by ample rainfall blanket the northern slopes of the mountains. On the southern slopes, the land is drier and features mixed wooded areas

Mongolians have been riding horses across the region's vast grassland for thousands of years.

Mongolia's Geographic Features

Area: 603,908 square miles (1,564,115 sq km)

Highest Elevation: Mount Huiten, 14,350 feet (4,374 m) above sea level

Lowest Elevation: Hoh Lake, 1,873 feet (570 m) above sea level

Longest River: Orkhon, about 700 miles (1,130 km) long

Deepest Lake: Hovsgol Lake, 860 feet (262 m)

Average High Temperature: In Ulaanbaatar, 4°F (−16°C) in January, 76°F (25°C) in July

Average Low Temperature: In Ulaanbaatar, −15°F (−26°C) in January, 55°F (13°C) in July

Average Annual Precipitation: In Ulaanbaatar, 11 inches (28 cm)

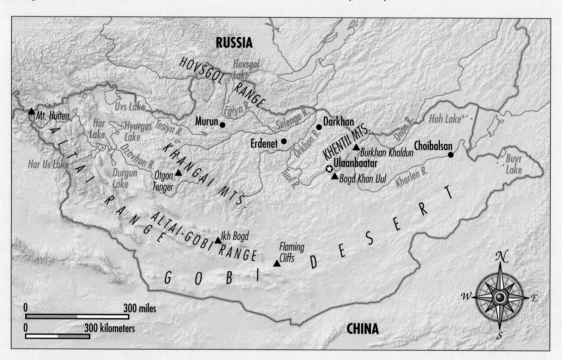

and grasslands. Eastern Mongolia is part of the Great Eurasian Steppe, a grassland that stretches from central Europe across Asia. Steppe landscapes are usually located between desert and forest. If steppe lands received more rain, they would be forest; if less rain fell, the steppe would become desert. The Mongolian steppe is important grazing land for livestock.

Singing Sands

The Gobi Desert has one of only a few dozen singing sands sites in the world. The site covers 115 miles (185 km) of the southern Gobi. Singing sands occur when wind or motion disturbs the sand and creates booming musical sounds.

Several specific conditions must be present for singing sands to occur. The sand must contain the material silica; the dunes must be at least 150 feet (45 m) tall; and the grains of sand must be small, of uniform size, and perfectly rounded. Most grains of sand are rough and jagged; round grains of sand are rare.

Additionally, the top layer of the sand dune must be very dry and loose, while the layer below must be hard-packed and somewhat damp. The wind or movement on the sand causes sound waves to ripple between the upper and lower layers. The hard, damp layer increases the volume of the vibrations. Singing sands ring out with the musical notes of E, F, or G.

Although Mongolia is remote, pollution is putting the singing sands at risk. Particles of air pollution can coat the grains of sand and quiet the beautiful sounds.

Desert

Although most of Mongolia is covered in mountains, for many people the name Mongolia brings to mind the Gobi Desert. About one-third of the country is desert, though not all of that is part of the Gobi. In fact, there are about thirty deserts in Mongolia besides the Gobi. The Gobi, however, is the largest desert in Asia. In Mongolia, it stretches more than 1,200 miles (1,900 km) across the eastern part of the country. The Gobi stretches beyond Mongolia's borders southward into the

Chinese region of Inner Mongolia and Tibet. Eighty million years ago, the Gobi was a rich grassland with lakes and streams, and was home to many species of dinosaurs. Volcanic activity and monumental dust and sand storms buried the dinosaurs and covered the land. The area became arid, but not all sand. Besides sand dunes, the Gobi contains rocky outcroppings, salty lakes, fertile oases, and mountains, some of which are covered in snow year-round. Underground streams called *gobs* (the origin of the desert's name) surface as freshwater springs, helping plants and animals survive. The desert also contains vast tracts of mineral deposits, including copper and gold.

The Orkhon River, the longest river in Mongolia, is quite shallow. Even in July and August, when the river is at its fullest, few boats are able to travel on it.

Rivers and Lakes

Mongolia's major rivers flow in the north and west. In the Altai Mountains, heat from within the earth warms many underground rivers. They emerge aboveground in the form of hot springs. Rivers flowing off the Altai flow into a massive depression, which contains many lakes, including Mongolia's largest lake, the salty Uvs Lake, which lies on the Russian border.

The Khentii range gives rise to three important rivers, the Onon, Kherlen, and Tuul. The Tuul River valley is home to the capital city of Ulaanbaatar and most of the country's

Blue Pearl

Formed approximately two to five million years ago, Hovsgol Lake is one of the oldest lakes in the world. It is Mongolia's deepest lake and holds nearly 2 percent of all the fresh water on the surface of the earth. It is located high in northern Mongolia, 5,397 feet (1,645 m) above sea level. Ninety-six rivers and streams flow into the lake and only one, the Egiyn River, flows out. The water of Hovsgol Lake is so pure and clear it is known as the Blue Pearl of Mongolia.

population. The Orkhon, Mongolia's longest river, rises in the Khangai Mountains.

Mongolia has more than 3,500 lakes. Most of them are shallow, salty, and located in the semidesert and desert regions. Major freshwater lakes include Hovsgol in the north and Hoh in the center of the country. Hoh Lake is Mongolia's lowest point at 1,873 feet (570 m) above sea level.

Climate

Mongolia has what is known as a continental climate, meaning that because of its distance from oceans and seas, its weather is not tempered by the sea air. As a result, Mongolia's weather is extreme. It has short, warm, wet summers and long, cold, dry winters. The northern mountains receive the most precipitation in the country, an average of about 12 inches (30 centimeters) per year, while in the southern desert areas, less than 8 inches (20 cm) falls. About two out of every three days in Mongolia, however, feature a clear, sunny sky.

Mongolia is one of the coldest countries on earth. Temperatures in Mongolia are coldest in the mountainous north, where temperatures have fallen as low as –67 degrees Fahrenheit (–55 degrees Celsius). Winters last from October to April. January is the coldest month, with an average temperature around the nation of –15°F (–26°C). Although winters are generally dry, some snow does fall. The most dramatic weather event in Mongolia is the fearsome *zud*—a winter with violent winds, snow, ice, and bitterly low temperatures. In such conditions, the grasslands freeze and deprive

Sheep and goats graze on grasses in the Gobi Desert.

grazing animals of their food source. A zud such as the one that occurred in 2010, when eight million livestock animals died, can destroy livelihoods.

Spring is an unpredictable time of year. Windstorms, sandstorms, or even snow can appear suddenly. Temperatures can vary wildly. Hot, summery days are sometimes followed by freezing nights. Summer brings welcome rain and the land comes alive with growing plants. Rivers race down mountainsides, and lakes become full. In mountainous regions, an average July high is about 68°F (20°C), while in valleys and steppe areas, highs average about 77°F (25°C). In the Gobi Desert, average summer temperatures range from 85°F to 95°F (30°C to 35°C). Many Mongolians consider autumn to be their favorite season. Temperatures and rainfall are moderate, and trees and grasslands turn brilliant red and gold.

A cloud of sand blows across the Gobi Desert. Sandstorms can make breathing difficult, kill young crops, and damage engines.

A Look at Mongolia's Cities

Mongolia's largest city is its capital, Ulaanbaatar, which had an estimated population of 1,226,991 in 2013. Erdenet (above), the second-largest city in Mongolia with a population of more than 80,000, is also one of the nation's newest cities. It was established in 1974 by the government of the Soviet Union (a country that has since split apart into Russia and many neighboring nations) when one of the world's largest deposits of copper was discovered. In its earliest days, nearly half the people in the community were Russian engineers and miners. The Soviets left Mongolia in the early 1990s, and now about 10 percent of the city's population is Russian. Today, the copper mine employs mostly Mongolian workers. In the city's town square stands a mining museum. The city also boasts a large carpet factory.

Darkhan, home to about 75,000, is the third-largest city in Mongolia. The Soviets built it as a manufacturing city in 1961, and it remains industrial. Darkhan is known for its Museum of Folk Art, which displays clothing, religious objects, and archaeological artifacts. The city also has a monument to the horsehead fiddle, the national instrument of Mongolia. Today, students from throughout Mongolia come to Darkhan to attend one of its many colleges, universities, and vocational schools.

Choibalsan, which has a population of about 40,000, was long named Bulgan Tumen. For hundreds of years, the site was a trading post, and in the nineteenth and early twentieth centuries it was the largest trading center in eastern Mongolia. In 1940, the Soviet government built a large military base there and renamed the city after Khorloogiin Choibalsan, a Mongolian communist leader. After the Soviet government abandoned the city and the military base in the early 1990s, the population fell drastically. Today, many citizens have returned to rural ways of making a living, and it is common to see people on camels passing through town.

Murun, with a population of about 35,000, is a northern Mongolian city and capital of its province, or *aimag*. The community was settled in the early nineteenth century around a Buddhist monastery. Before the arrival of the Soviet government, there were more than one thousand lamas (Buddhist holy men) in residence. The Soviets dismantled the monastery, but it was rebuilt after they departed. Although small, the city has a hospital, a museum, a theater, and several schools. In 2015, a paved road connecting it to Ulaanbaatar was completed.

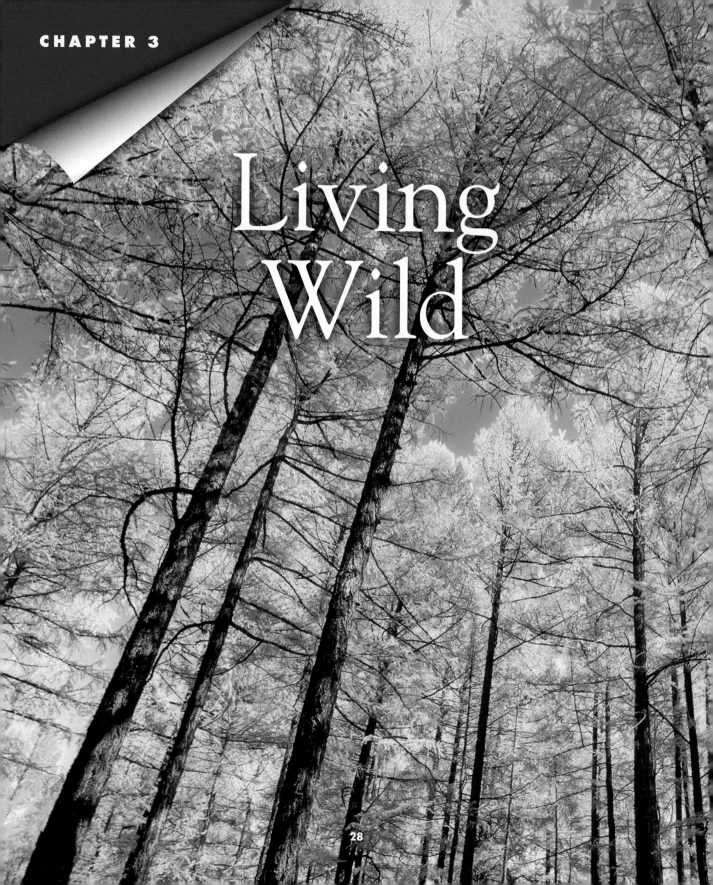

CHAPTER 3

Living Wild

MONGOLIA IS ONE OF THE LAST UNSPOILED places on earth. From the northern mountains, through forests and river valleys, across wild grasslands, to vast desert sands, the various landforms in Mongolia make homes for a wide variety of plant and animal life. Many plants and wildlife in Mongolia live nowhere else in the world.

Being Green

Within Mongolia's differing regions, a remarkable variety of plants, flowers, grasses, and trees can be found. Low population, clean air, pure water, and relatively little human development allow many plant species to thrive.

Forests cover nearly 15 percent of the country. The northernmost taiga forests are dense with stands of Siberian pines and east Siberian larches—conifers (cone-bearing trees) whose needles turn brilliant red and drop to the ground in autumn. Mosses and lichens are found growing on trees and

Alpine asters hug the dry soil on the Mongolian steppe.

rocks in the high altitudes. On the north side of the hills and mountains of the mountain-steppe zone grow larches, aspens, Siberian spruces, and Mongolian Scots pines. Where there are rocky slopes, the Japanese stone pine grows. In lower elevations grow leafy trees such as poplars, willows, and Mongolian oaks. Low-lying bushes such as rhododendrons, blackberries, blueberries, and currants thrive on the forest floor.

Steppes and grassland cover more than 50 percent of the Mongolian landscape. In rockier areas grow small trees and shrubs such as dragon spruces and Turkestan junipers. Siberian elms are very drought and cold resistant and offer welcome windbreaks and shade to animals and herders on the steppe. Native rhubarb grows in abundance on the steppe, as does Russian thistle, or tumbleweed. Besides a wide variety of tough, cold-resistant grasses, the steppe is a sea of color in spring and summer when abundant wildflowers bloom, including irises, lilies, geraniums, delphiniums, edelweiss, sweet peas, wild roses, asters, buttercups, and morning glories. Many wildflowers native to Mongolia have been collected by botanists and planted in flower gardens around the world.

The Gobi Desert and nearby semidesert lands are harsh environments, yet some plants defy the challenges of extreme temperatures and lack of water. Wild garlic, wormwood, and wild onion grow in the semidesert, as do various grasses. Reedy

Parts of the Gobi Desert are completely barren. In other parts, grasses can survive.

grasses and small flowering ivies can be found growing near shallow ponds and oases. Salty soils and marshes also support plant life, including pennywort, ranunculus, salt cedar, and saltwort, a weedy plant that grows in salty areas of the Gobi where other plants cannot grow. By far the most important plant of the Gobi and other dry regions is the saxaul tree. The leaves of the tree are so tiny that from a distance the tree looks barren, but in spring small yellow flowers are visible. The saxaul tree collects and stores water in its bark. Desert-dwelling animals and desert travelers can get water from the tree by squeezing the bark. The tree has deep roots to keep it upright against the wind, as well as another root system that extends outward. These outward-growing roots keep soil from eroding.

Creatures Big and Small

Mongolia is home to nearly 140 species of mammals, about ten types of amphibians, and twenty-two species of reptiles. Many of these species are endemic, meaning they live nowhere else. Three thousand kinds of insects and roughly 450 species of birds are also found in Mongolia.

Fields of Blue

On October 25, 2014, Mongolia declared scabiosa butterfly blue the national flower. The flower blooms all over Mongolia for three months each summer. It is resistant to drought and can survive the cold. Traditionally, Mongolian artisans have decorated saddles with scabiosa butterfly blue designs.

Leopard in Danger

Snow leopards live in cold, dry regions and amid rough terrain such as cliffs and icy ravines. Their spotted gray-on-white fur provides camouflage to help the animals surprise their prey, which includes wild sheep and goats, as well as smaller creatures such as hares.

Snow leopards are highly endangered, with fewer than six thousand of the animals left in the world. Despite the snow leopard being a top predator in Mongolia, its survival is at risk. Poaching, or illegal hunting, is a major problem. People who live in the snow leopard's habitat have few economic resources, and killing a snow leopard brings great financial rewards. Any snow leopard killed will attract willing buyers from all over the world. The snow leopard's bones and organs are in demand for certain Chinese medicines, and some people will pay thousands of dollars for the luxury of owning a snow leopard pelt.

Snow leopards also face danger because they sometimes stray into more populated areas and attack livestock. Herders then take revenge and shoot them. More and more, snow leopards are losing their habitat to human development, as mining areas, farms, and grazing areas expand. Governments and conservationists are working to come up with ways to protect these magnificent creatures.

Most of Mongolia's wild animals live in the mountains and northern forests. Besides the typical animals that dwell in cold climates, such as musk deer, moose, brown bear, and reindeer, Mongolia is also home to some of the world's rarest animals, such as lynx, argali sheep, ibex, and snow leopards.

The saiga antelope's large, flexible nose enables it to filter out dust that is kicked up as it runs through the dry Mongolian landscape.

In the forests of Mongolia live elk, wolf, roe deer, badgers, foxes, and wolves. The Mongolian marmot lives in burrows and dashes madly across the open steppe to escape predators, especially humans. Highly prized for its meat and pelt, the marmot, a large member of the squirrel family, has long been hunted.

The Mongolian saiga antelope lives on the steppe. It is notable for its great humped nose, which filters dust and circulates air so that the animal is cooled in summer and heated in winter. Other creatures of the steppe include Pallas's cats, wild boars, marbled polecats, Corsac foxes, and elks. The steppe-dwelling Mongolian gazelle is a fast runner and strong swimmer. During the spring, gazelles gather in large herds, sometimes made up of as many as six thousand animals, and migrate to different feeding grounds, traveling up to 125 miles (200 km) per day.

The steppe-desert regions and the Gobi Desert itself are home to many animals, from swift gazelles to the small and extremely rare Gobi bear. This bear survives on a spare diet of leaves, roots, insects, and an occasional lizard or mouse. The Gobi bear is one of the most endangered animals in the world. Fewer than forty are left in the wild. Many of the most commonly seen animals of the steppe and desert were historically wild species, but they have been domesticated, or tamed. These include wild donkeys, wild horses, wild sheep, yaks, and Bactrian (two-humped) camels.

Taking Wing

Mongolia is home to hundreds of species of birds. About three-quarters of the species migrate. Some make brief stopovers on their flights from southern regions to Siberia and northern Europe, while others remain for the summer to raise their young. Many birds in Mongolia flit from region to region, from mountain to steppe to desert to wetland. Grasslands abound

Spirit Horses

The *takhi*, which means "spirit" in Mongolian, is the last remaining species of wild horse. Wild horses in other regions of the world are actually feral, meaning that they come from domesticated ancestors, but live in the wild. The takhi is small, with thick legs and a powerful neck. In the 1880s, a Russian explorer identified the takhi as a wild horse and soon North American and European zoos and horse breeders hurried to add Mongolian wild horses to their collections. Many takhi were captured or died in transport, and by the 1960s, takhi horses became extinct in the wild. In 1997, horse breeders and scientists introduced a group of takhi into a protected area called the Valley of the Horses, in the northern Gobi Desert. Since then, the wild takhi horse has bred in the wild and the population is healthy and growing.

The Hunter

The national bird of Mongolia is the mighty saker falcon, a large bird of prey with a wingspan of about 4 feet (1.2 m). The saker falcon often nests in old nests made by other birds. It scouts for prey in grasslands, deserts, and steppes, diving at speeds of up to 200 miles per hour (320 kph) while hunting for hamsters, squirrels, hares, frogs, chipmunks, and other birds. The saker falcon was selected the national bird in 2012 because Mongolia has a long tradition of falconry—training falcons to assist in hunting—and the saker falcon has exceptional hunting skills.

The toad-headed agama is the most common reptile in the Gobi Desert.

with pheasants, quails, swallows, warblers, buntings, and larks. Forests and mountains are host to ravens, woodpeckers, and owls. Ducks, ibises, loons, swans, and storks can be found near

rivers and lakes, as can birds that often live along coasts, such as plovers, sandpipers, terns, pelicans, and gulls.

Amphibians, Reptiles, and Fish

Relatively few amphibian or reptile species live in Mongolia. There are toads, lizards, and geckos. Snakes found in the steppe and desert include the Gobi racerunner, the steppes rat snake, the Tatary sand boa, and the Asian viper. Dozens of species of fish swim the rivers and lakes, including kinds of trout, perch, and pike. One of the most notable species in Mongolia is the giant taimen, a type of freshwater salmon that can grow 6 feet (2 m) long.

Conservation

Mongolia has more than 60 million acres (20 million hectares) of protected land, such as national parks. The government recognizes the importance of protecting the nation's unique environment. Khorgo-Terkhiin Tsagaan Nuur National Park was established in 1965. An area of mountains and volcanic lakes, it is home to swans, cormorants, terns, ducks, and cranes, including the endangered white-naped crane. High in the Altai Mountains is Tavan Bogd National Park, where snow leopards and argali sheep live. The Hustai National Park protects habitat for the takhi horse and the Asiatic red deer, steppe gazelle, boar, wolf, and lynx. Gobi Gurvansaikhan

The white-naped crane is a large bird, standing about 4 feet (1.2 m) tall. It breeds in northeastern Mongolia and then migrates south for the winter.

National Park is Mongolia's largest national park, covering 6 million acres (2 million ha), an area about the size of the U.S. state of New Hampshire. It protects sand dunes, the Flaming Cliffs, canyons, glaciers, and animals such wolves, ibex, snow leopards, and Gobi bears.

Both male and female ibex have horns, but the males' horns are much larger.

Off-Limits

Mongolia is home to the world's first national conservation area. During the mid-1500s, the Ming dynasty established protections for the Bogd Khan Uul region, citing the mountain's beauty and sacred nature. In 1778, the Mongolian government officially declared the area off-limits to poachers, hunters, miners, and anyone inclined to disturb the area's peace and beauty. More than 2,000 lamas living in a nearby monastery and armed with clubs were deputized to protect the mountain. The monastery was destroyed in the 1930s, but part of it has been rebuilt and is now a museum (left).

CHAPTER 4

March Through Time

ARLY HUMANS LIVED IN WHAT IS NOW MONGOLIA more than two million years ago. These people made tools from rock and bone. Archaeologists have found the remains of 750,000-year-old stone tools in caves in southwestern Mongolia. Between 100,000 and 40,000 years ago, modern humans moved into Mongolia. They knew how to make fire and communicated by carving pictures and symbols on stone outcroppings and cave walls. The climate grew colder during this period, and glaciers moved through the region. Humans sought refuge from the ice in sheltered valleys and caves.

Opposite: **Carved stones erected by ancient Mongolians date to the second century BCE.**

Developing Culture

When the ice retreated, between 40,000 and 10,000 years ago, human society advanced further. Humans began crafting movable homes. They made round structures of hides and wool, called *gers*, or yurts. Carved rock paintings, or petroglyphs, from this time depict humans hunting giant mammoths

Ancient Mongolians drew deer and other animals on rocks across northern Mongolia.

and rhinoceroses. In the centuries that followed, people in Mongolia developed the bow and arrow and more often lived in dwellings along rivers and in valleys. Mongolian culture developed rapidly. The people improved tools, raised grain crops, made pottery, decorated household items, and domesticated wild animals. Later, the people began making metal arrowheads, knives, and swords. With the advanced technology of metal weapons, Mongolian groups became nomadic hunters, following herds of wild animals. They hunted the animals for food and to use the bones, hides, and fur to make tools, clothing, and shelter. By the seventh century BCE, Mongolians had established a nomadic way of life that in some parts of the country exists to this day.

When Mongolians domesticated animals, they went from being nomadic hunters to nomadic farmers and herders. Rather than following wild animal herds, nomadic herders began guiding their animals to camps at seasonal grazing grounds. In winter, they set up their camps in sheltered valleys and mountainside caves. In summer, they sought lush, open grasslands. Some nomads became farmers and grew crops for their animals.

Ancient Empires and Khanates

The earliest recorded mentions of Mongolia are in Chinese texts, which describe the Mongolians as the Hu, meaning "primitives," and the Xiongnu, meaning "vassals." Raids were frequent, and in 221 BCE, the Chinese Qin dynasty began constructing and fortifying walls to fend off Mongolian invaders. The walls, meant to stop horses, not men, eventually became the Great Wall of China.

The Five Snouts

Likely there has been no greater influence on Mongolian life than the people's relationship to domesticated animals. For thousands of years, Mongolians have raised the "five snouts": horses, sheep, goats, cows, and camels. Of the five snouts, the horse reigns supreme. Taming the wild horse gave Mongolians the ability to move about quickly and to carry their belongings. The Mongolian nomads designed a horse-drawn sleigh that transported their household goods, tools, food, clothing, and dwellings. Around 500 BCE, Mongolian metalworkers developed the stirrup (left). This invention allowed hunters on horseback to stand as they rode so that they could turn and shoot arrows in many directions.

Counting by Tens

Modu Chanyu was the first leader to create a united Mongolian state. A cunning strategist, he began building an empire by conquering neighboring nomadic groups. His ultimate goal was to conquer China.

He was aware that his groups of nomadic warriors were too independent and disorganized to be effective, so he designed an organization scheme that would go on to benefit future Mongolian empires and influence military organizations around the world.

Modu Chanyu assigned soldiers to squadrons of ten thousand men. These squadrons were divided into units of one thousand men, one hundred men, and ten men. Each leader of ten was typically a local chief, who was already respected by the soldiers who served under him. The leaders of the other groups reported to the larger group above them. With 240,000 soldiers at his command, Modu Chanyu conquered the Chinese Qin dynasty and signed a peace treaty with its successors, the Han dynasty. Modu Chanyu's Xiongnu Empire prospered until 47 BCE.

In the fourth century, a nomadic group from eastern Mongolia took over the Xiongnu Empire and parts of northern China. It became known as the Northern Wei dynasty. The nomads settled down and adopted many Chinese ways, including fortifying the Great Wall against their own people. However, by 400 CE, nomadic groups in central Mongolia began to unite and eventually expanded to rule over an area from the Pacific Ocean to west of what is now Mongolia. The rulers of this empire were the first to be called "khan."

In 552, Turkic people in western Mongolia rebelled against the ruling khan and added Mongolia to the great Turkic Khanate, Asia's most powerful nomadic empire. In 741, the Uighurs, a Turkic people, took control of what is now Mongolia and allied themselves with China. At first, they brought peace to the region. They translated Chinese texts and developed Mongolia's first written language. But later in their rule, they attacked the Kyrgyz people to the north and the Tibetans to the south. The Kyrgyz fought back and defeated the Uighurs.

After the fall of the Uighur Khanate, an eastern Mongolian nomadic group called the Khitan rose to power, taking over much of what is now Mongolia and northern China. The Khitan, inspired by the Chinese, who were not nomadic, built more than 150 cities, fortresses, and temples.

The Great Khans

By the early twelfth century, the Khitan Khanate in Mongolia had mostly disbanded. Without the Khitan Khanate to keep order, various groups fell into fierce rivalries. Leaders of different clans, or groups of related families, vied for control. A leader named Yesugei was poisoned, and his wife and children were banished to the wilderness. They survived, and the youngest son swore revenge. He formed many alliances as he worked his way up to become a khan of his tribal group. By 1206, the young man had gained control of a vast swath of land, from Lake Baikal in southern Russia to the Great Wall. He named his khanate "Mongol Uls," meaning the "people of the state." Soon, a gathering of leaders named the young man Chinggis Khan (sometimes called Genghis Khan), meaning "universal ruler."

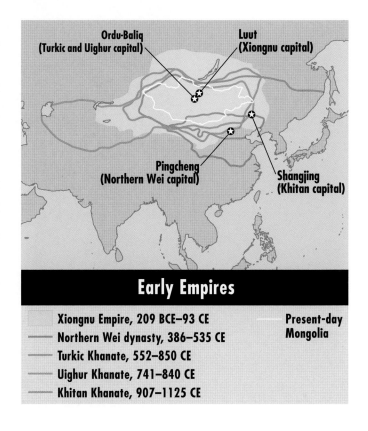

Early Empires

Xiongnu Empire, 209 BCE–93 CE
Northern Wei dynasty, 386–535 CE
Turkic Khanate, 552–850 CE
Uighur Khanate, 741–840 CE
Khitan Khanate, 907–1125 CE

Present-day Mongolia

Ordu-Baliq (Turkic and Uighur capital)
Luut (Xiongnu capital)
Pingcheng (Northern Wei capital)
Shangjing (Khitan capital)

Chinggis Khan immediately stood out as a ruler. He formed a large, central government, which produced a code of law. Unlike the leaders of many empires, he had no interest in imposing Mongol religious beliefs on the lands the Mongols controlled. Instead, he let these regions continue to practice their own religions. Chinggis Khan also developed a complex system of communication. Using five thousand way stations,

Chinggis Khan ruled the Mongol Empire for more than twenty years.

Chinggis Khan leads troops across the steppe. Mongol soldiers were typically armed with bows and arrows, lances, and swords.

messengers rode on horseback in relays to deliver messages. Chinggis Khan built a highly effective and highly organized army. He developed new battle strategies, attacking by surprise, at night, or in the dead of winter. He often attacked by spreading his army units wide apart. These units used horns, flags, and his messenger system to communicate. The Mongols did not kill or enslave the best enemy warriors; instead, these warriors were forced to join Chinggis's army, and many became generals. Chinggis also hired military engineers who developed weapons such as catapults to hurl rocks, supports to aid in throwing javelins, and machines that sent burning stakes into the air.

A New Look at an Old Leader

Mongolians acknowledge that, to much of the world, the name Chinggis Khan brings to mind images of brutal warfare, but this is an incomplete image of the man. In Mongolia, people take pride in his leadership skills, accomplishments, written code of laws, and ability to unify a vast and much divided country. Mongolians now honor Chinggis Khan as the founder of their nation.

In 2013, Sukhbaatar Square, the center of Ulaanbaatar, was renamed after Chinggis Khan and a marble and bronze statue of him was erected. The airport in Ulaanbaatar is named after him, as is a major university. About 34 miles (55 km) outside of Ulaanbaatar is the world's largest equestrian statue (right), which depicts Chinggis Khan leading a charge on horseback. The steel statue is 130 feet (40 m) tall and stands atop a visitors' center devoted to Mongolia's mightiest ruler.

Before his death, Chinggis Khan divided the empire into four khanates. Chinggis's grandson Batu, and later his offspring, ruled a khanate that became known as the Golden Horde. The Golden Horde controlled the western part of the Mongol Empire, covering much of Russia, central Asia, and as far west as Poland and Hungary. In the mid-1200s, the Golden Horde swept across the Middle East. They killed many thousands of people in Baghdad, the most powerful city in the Middle East and a center of learning. Many of the people conquered by the Golden Horde, including most of those in the Middle East, were Muslims, people who followed the religion Islam.

aquesta caravana es partida del imperi
de sarra p mar calatayo:

camul

solar

fichar

The Silk Road

The Silk Road was a system of trade routes that connected Eastern and Western civilizations. Europeans sought luxury goods produced in India, China, Persia, and Southeast Asia. Traders were sent to buy goods such as silk, gems, spices, perfumes, and glassware. They bought Chinese pottery, Indian cloth, and Persian carpets. In exchange, the Europeans sent wool, horses, and wine to Asia, while North African societies sent ivory and gold.

There were many different routes along the Silk Road. In China, Mongolia, and central Asia, the paths led across deserts and over treacherous mountain ranges. Most traders rode camels in groups called caravans, and besides the challenges of terrain, they were also at the mercy of bandits. In the thirteenth century, Chinggis Khan established thousands of tollbooths, where he demanded "passports" and charged taxes for safe passage. These taxes were a major source of funding for his military exploits.

The leaders of the four khanates did not always agree on how to keep the empire strong. China was a major issue among the different Mongol groups. All agreed that keeping China under Mongolian control was vital, yet they disagreed on how much influence Chinese culture should have on Mongolia. Kublai Khan, Chinggis's grandson, was well educated and was inclined toward China, a country that was advanced in language, arts, and science. He moved the Mongolian capital to what is now Beijing, China. In 1276, Kublai Khan's forces put all of China under Mongol control. He established the Yuan

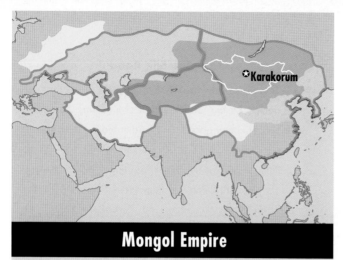

Mongol Empire

Growth of the Mongol Empire, 1227–1259:

- Mongol Empire, 1227
- Lands added by 1241
- Lands added by 1259
- Present-day Mongolia

Divisions of the Mongol Empire, 1294:

- Empire of the Great Khan
- Khanate of the Golden Horde
- Ilkhan Khanate
- Chagatai Khanate

(meaning "first") dynasty. Under Kublai Khan, the Mongol Empire spread over more than 12 million square miles (31 million square kilometers) of territory throughout Asia and Europe, making it the largest land-based empire in history.

Kublai Khan surrounded himself in luxury. The great khan was a great supporter of science, trade, education, and the fine arts. He introduced paper money and ordered scholars to devise a written Mongolian language, in part based on Chinese writing. He improved and expanded trade by building seaports, shipping canals, bridges, and better

Women in the Mongol Empire

During the time of the great khans, women in Mongolia had more rights than women in other parts of the world. They could own and inherit property. The family ger, for example, typically was the property of a woman. Mongol society desired strength and independence among women, and some became political and military leaders.

Sorghaghtani Beki was one of the most powerful figures in the Mongol Empire. A great political figure who held significant power, she raised her four sons, including Kublai Khan, to be leaders. Sorghaghtani Beki promoted religious tolerance within the empire and encouraged trade throughout the land.

To the East

In the late 1200s, two Italian merchants, Niccolo and Maffeo Polo brought Marco, Niccolo's son, on a journey to Kublai Khan's court. The expedition took four years. It was a physical challenge and an intellectual eye-opener for the young man. He experienced not only the vast landscapes of soaring mountains and vast deserts, but the vast differences between European and Asian cultures. When Marco Polo (near left) arrived at the grand summer palace of Kublai Khan (far left) in Xanadu (now Shangdu, China), he was astounded by its magnificence. Marco Polo spent seventeen years in Kublai Khan's court. He learned four languages and became a member of the khan's high council. After returning to Italy, he wrote his now-famous book, *The Travels of Marco Polo*.

roads. Kublai Khan's rule was a time of peace and prosperity, when Eastern and Western societies shared goods and ideas.

Despite being prosperous under Kublai Khan, some Mongolians resented the influence of Chinese culture. Fighting between different groups intensified. In the mid-fourteenth century, Chinese rebels ousted the Mongolian rulers. The Chinese then refused to trade goods such as silk, iron, and grains with Mongolia. Mongolian groups returned to self-sufficiency by herding, fishing, and farming.

By the early fifteenth century, Mongolian society had become deeply divided. Fierce battles broke out between the central and eastern khanates, the western khanate from the Altai Mountains, and the khanates who claimed their khan was a direct descendant of Chinggis Khan. In 1543, Altan Khan led the eastern Mongols on a raid of the Ming dynasty. After failing to conquer the Chinese, he returned to his homeland and established a stable government. Altan Khan was a religious man who introduced Buddhism to Mongolia, and in 1578, he named his Buddhist teacher, Sonam Gyatso, the Dalai Lama, which in Mongolian means "one whose wisdom is as deep as the ocean."

In the 1500s, the Mongolian people were again at the mercy of dozens of warring khanates. Many of the khanates in

Altan Khan was central to the spread of Buddhism in Mongolia.

Mandukhai the Wise

In 1465, nineteen-year-old Mandukhai married Manduul Khan and became khatun, or queen. The two did not have a child to succeed them. The khan was an older man and as he neared the end of his life, many sought to take his throne and marry the khatun. When the khan died, Mandukhai Khatun refused all suitors and instead adopted a small boy who was a direct descendant of Chinggis Khan. Meanwhile, all of Mongolia's khanates were seeking control of Mongolia. Knowing that it would be a challenge for Mongolians to accept a small boy as the great khan, Mandukhai Khatun explained that the boy, whom she named Dayan Khan, was the rightful heir to the throne and that she would protect and guide him until he was of age to rule on his own. She promised that no harm would come to the Mongolian people under her guidance, or the people could "break and rip apart [her] body." The khatun did as she promised. She herself successfully led warriors into battle and took central control over the warring khanates. When the boy was of age, they married and together ruled over a unified Mongolia.

the west had allied themselves with the rulers of Tibet, to the southwest, and in 1636, sixteen eastern khans surrendered to Manchuria, in what is now northeastern China. Chinese leaders of the Ming dynasty saw these divisions as an opening, so they attacked Mongolia. Some Mongolian khanates remained loyal to the Chinese emperor. But the Manchu armies and their Mongolian allies eventually overtook the Ming dynasty. Manchu rulers renamed themselves the Qing dynasty and ruled over China and Mongolia until 1911.

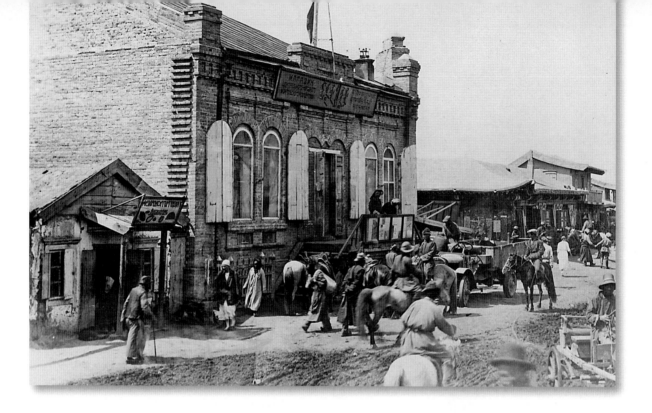

A department store in Urga, now Ulaanbaatar, in 1920. At the time, the city was home to about sixty thousand people.

Enter Russia

In the late seventeenth and early eighteenth centuries, China and Russia signed treaties defining the borders of Mongolia. It was at this time that the regions called Inner Mongolia and Outer Mongolia emerged. Eastern groups lived in Inner Mongolia and northern and western groups lived in Outer Mongolia. Initially, both regions were part of China. Russia and China distrusted each other, however, so as the Qing dynasty weakened, Russia encouraged Mongolia to declare independence. Inner Mongolia stayed loyal to China, but Outer Mongolia declared its independence in 1911. In 1919, however, Chinese troops recaptured Outer Mongolia.

During that period, Russia had experienced a revolution and become a communist country. Russians who opposed this change were known as White Russians. Mongolian leaders invited the White Russian army to help drive the Chinese out of Mongolia. In 1921, Mongolia declared independence once again. But soon after, Mongolian leaders felt White Russian rule was just as oppressive as Chinese rule. So Mongolia again sought aid. By this time, Russia and other nearby states had become the Union of Soviet Socialist Republics (USSR). Mongolia became one of the USSR's satellite states, a nation that is technically independent but is under the political, economic, and military control of another country. In 1924, Mongolia renamed itself the Mongolian People's Republic. For the next seventy years, it had a communist government under Soviet control.

The Red Hero

At the heart of Ulaanbaatar lies a vast concrete and marble square once named after Damdin Sukhbaatar, a revolutionary hero who was drafted into the army when Mongolia declared independence from China in 1911. But a few years later, when Mongolia was back under Chinese rule, Sukhbaatar joined a secret group that hoped to convince the Russian army to help the Mongolians defeat the Chinese. Mongolian leader Bogd Khan gave Sukhbaatar a message to give to Russian leaders, which he carried in the hollow handle of his horsewhip. After receiving the message, Russian troops came to the rescue and helped liberate Mongolia from Chinese occupation.

In 1924, the square in the center of the city was named Sukhbaatar Square. The city itself was renamed after him—Ulaanbaatar means "Red Hero," and the Soviet army was known as the Red Army. After his death, a statue was erected in the square in his honor. He is mounted on his horse with his hand raised. The inscription reads: "If we, an entire people unite in common effort and common will, there is nothing in the world we cannot achieve, learn, and succeed in."

The Soviet Union dominated Mongolia through most of the twentieth century. Here, a ceremony celebrating the Russian Revolution is held in Ulaanbaatar in 1962.

Between 1930 and 1940, thousands of Mongolian men, who the USSR said threatened national stability, were murdered or exiled to the barren, frozen lands of Siberia. Buddhist monks, other religious leaders, artists, and intellectuals suffered similar fates. In 1936, Soviet leader Joseph Stalin ordered the destruction of countless historic buildings, houses of worship, statues, and religious monuments in Mongolia.

The Soviet Union also improved some aspects of life in Mongolia. It introduced modern transportation and communication systems, improved health and education, and installed running water and wastewater systems. Many Mongolian students were sent to the Soviet Union for an advanced education in science, engineering, and medicine. Additionally, the Soviet government established cities, built factories, opened mines, and funded new and better schools.

These advancements improved the livelihoods of many Mongolian people. But then, facing political and economic

The Last Great Khan

The last great khan of Mongolia, Bogd Khan, was born in 1869 to a family of Tibetan nobles. When the boy was four years old, Tibetan Buddhist religious leaders said he was a reincarnation of the fourth-most important Buddhist lama, or spiritual master. The child lived in a monastery until moving to Mongolia, in 1874, where he was acknowledged as Mongolia's spiritual leader.

Although Tibetan by birth, Bogd Khan was determined to see Mongolia become independent. In 1911, after the defeat of the Qing dynasty, he was declared the great khan of Mongolia. During his short reign, nearly one-seventh of all Mongolian men were lamas living in monasteries. These religious men did not work, but rather begged for a living, relying on contributions from others. During this time, there was a shortage of men to participate in the military, as well as a shortage of workers. The lack of a strong military and a weak economy helped the Chinese regain control of Mongolia. After the Chinese were again driven out, Bogd Khan regained his authority. But later, when the USSR gained control, he retained only a ceremonial role.

troubles of its own, the Soviet Union retreated from Mongolia. A depression struck, as schools, railroads, and industries were abandoned overnight.

Choibalsan was a thriving town under Soviet rule, with a population of nearly three hundred thousand people. The city had industry, schools, and a military base. But in 1990, without mentioning anything to Mongolian officials, the Soviet residents of Choibalsan evacuated the town in just a few hours. All at once, an entire commercial center collapsed. Factories ceased to operate, and workers were without

Mongolians fill Sukhbaatar Square in 1990 to show their support for the new government.

jobs. The power plant shut down, and people were forced to ransack former Soviet homes for wood to burn for fuel. Once a bustling city, Choibalsan today still struggles to survive, jobs are few, housing and public services are inadequate, and the nearest paved road outside of the city center is 185 miles (300 km) away. Sadly, this fate was not limited to Choibalsan; many of Mongolia's manufacturing towns fared no better.

Recent Times

In the late 1980s, the Soviet Union was undergoing major change, as people challenged communism and one-party rule. In Mongolia, similar disruptions were afoot. On December 10, 1989, thousands of demonstrators gathered in Sukhbaatar Square in the capital of Ulaanbaatar. They called for an end to Soviet rule and demanded democratic elections. Several new political parties formed, and in 1990 the Soviet government retreated from Mongolia. On February 12, 1992, Mongolia became an independent country. Later that year, Mongolia held its first free elections. The communist party, the Mongolian People's Revolutionary Party (MPRP), won the elections. In years after, however, control of Mongolia shifted between communists, socialists, and democrats.

Mongolia's economy has had many ups and downs in recent times, including a great recession, or economic decline, in the 1990s. Mongolians have also had to work to rebuild and rediscover the culture that was damaged by hundreds of years of rule by outsiders. Mongolians are independent and resourceful, and with gains in Mongolia's economy and greater access to world markets and ideas, citizens foresee a bright future.

In recent years, Ulaanbaatar has grown rapidly. Its population more than doubled in the first twenty years after the Soviets left Mongolia.

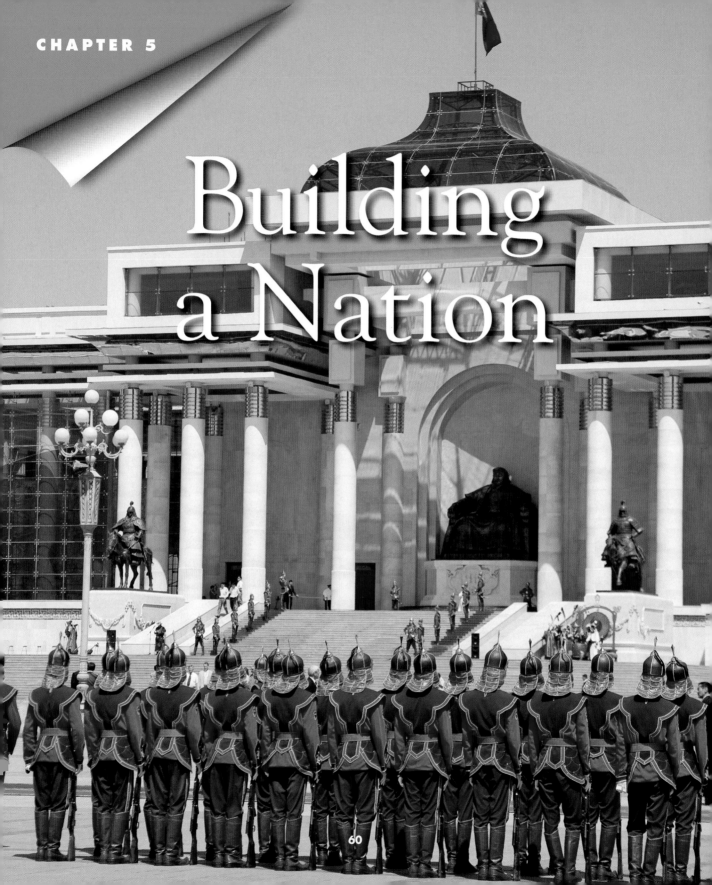

CHAPTER 5

Building a Nation

THE MONGOLIAN GOVERNMENT DRAFTED ITS PRESENT constitution in 1992 and amended it in 2002. Mongolia's previous constitutions, from the mid-twentieth century, were modeled after the Soviet Union's constitution. They gave unlimited power to the communist party and restricted freedom of speech, the press, and religion, and the right to assemble. Mongolia's 1992 constitution did away with one-party rule and emphasized human rights, property rights, freedom of speech, and other individual freedoms. The constitution also established three branches of government—executive, legislative, and judicial.

The Executive Branch

The president is the head of the executive branch of government. He or she is elected by the people to a four-year term and can run for a second term. The president acts as head of state, serving as the face of government and representing Mongolia

Mongolian prime minister Chimediin Saikhanbileg (left) shakes hands with Japanese prime minister Shinzo Abe after the two signed a trade agreement in 2015.

in foreign affairs. The president also acts as commander in chief of the armed forces, signs bills into law, appoints diplomats to foreign countries, and recommends candidates for prime minister. The president must be at least forty-five years old and a native-born Mongolian.

The head of government is the prime minister. Members of the parliament, called the Mongolian Great Khural, select the prime minister, who usually comes from the majority political party. The prime minister, in consultation with the president, appoints cabinet ministers who oversee major government departments, such as justice, labor, energy, agriculture, and finance.

Mongolia's National Government

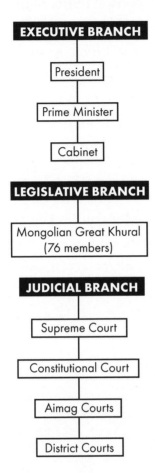

EXECUTIVE BRANCH

President

Prime Minister

Cabinet

LEGISLATIVE BRANCH

Mongolian Great Khural
(76 members)

JUDICIAL BRANCH

Supreme Court

Constitutional Court

Aimag Courts

District Courts

Legislative Branch

Mongolia's legislative branch of government consists of the Mongolian Great Khural. It is a unicameral legislature, meaning that there is only one house. The Great Khural has seventy-six seats. Forty-eight members are elected directly by the people. Citizens also vote for political parties, and the remaining twenty-eight members of the Great Khural are chosen to represent their party in proportion to the number of votes their party received. All members of the parliament serve four-year terms.

The chief role of the Great Khural is to enact new laws and amend or remove former laws. Members of parliament can also vote to dismiss the prime minister. The largest parties represented in the Great Khural are the Mongolian People's Party and the Democratic Party.

Judicial Branch

The highest court in Mongolia is the Supreme Court, which consists of a chief justice and twenty-four other justices. They preside over three chambers—civil, criminal, and administra-

A meeting of the Mongolian Great Khural. In 2015, women accounted for 15 percent of the members of parliament.

The National Flag

The national flag of Mongolia consists of a rectangle divided vertically into three equal parts. The left and right stripes are red, symbolizing progress and prosperity. The center stripe is blue, standing for Mongolia's eternal blue sky. On the red stripe nearest the flagpole is a golden symbol called the *soyombo*, which derives from a seventeenth century Mongolian script. The characters in the soyombo have the following meanings: The three tongues of flame stand for the past, present, and future. The sun and moon are symbols of growth, wealth, and success. The two downward-pointing triangles represent an arrow indicating the defeat of Mongolia's enemies. The two horizontal rectangles sym-bolize equality for all. The circular yin-yang symbol indicates the unity of opposing forces. The two vertical rectangles suggest the walls of a fort, representing the strength of the Mongolian people.

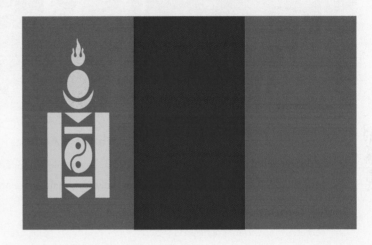

tive. The president appoints the justices on recommendation from the Great Khural. The Supreme Court hears important cases and reviews decisions made in lower courts.

Mongolia also has a Constitutional Court, which determines whether laws are constitutional. The Constitutional Court has nine judges, three appointed by the president, three appointed by the Great Khural, and three appointed by the Supreme Court. The judges serve six-year terms.

District courts handle most civil and criminal cases. Aimag (provincial) courts hear more serious cases and review the decisions of lower courts. Ulaanbaatar also has its own court system, which includes civil, criminal, and administrative divisions.

National Anthem

Mongolia's national anthem was adopted in 1950. Zewegmiddiin Gaitaw wrote the music, and Tsendiin Damdinsüren wrote the words. The lyrics have changed over the years, removing mention of communist leaders.

English translation

Our sacred independent country
Is the ancestral hearth of all Mongols,
May all of the world's good deeds
Prosper and continue for eternity.

Our country will strengthen relations
With all righteous countries of the world.
And let us develop our beloved Mongolia
With all our will and might.

Our great nation's symbol blesses us
And the people's fate supports us
Let us pass on our ancestry, culture and language
From generation to generation

The brilliant people of the brave Mongolia
Have gained freedom and happiness,
The key to delight, and the path to progress,
Majestic Mongolia—our country, live forever.

Local Government

Mongolia has twenty-two administrative districts. These include the capital city district of Ulaanbaatar and twenty-one *aimags*, or provinces. Each province is led by a governor, who is appointed by the prime minister, and each province also has a local assembly, whose members are elected to four-year terms.

A Look at Ulaanbaatar

People have lived on the site of what is now the capital of Ulaanbaatar for hundreds of thousands of years. The city itself was founded in 1639 as a nomadic monastery. The city, often called Urga at the time, attracted ten thousand monks and became a major monastic center. By the 1700s, it was a major trading center between Russia and China. In 1924, the city's name was changed to Ulaanbaatar. Today, Ulaanbaatar is growing by leaps and bounds as people move in from the countryside. Its population in 2013 was 1,226,991.

Buildings in Ulaanbaatar include a mixture of Russian, Tibetan, Chinese, and Mongolian styles with modern touches. There are also glass skyscrapers, such as the Chinggis Khaan Hotel.

Ulaanbaatar has many excellent museums. The Zanabazar Museum of Fine Arts has an outstanding collection of paintings and sculptures from ancient times to the present. Many visitors are drawn to the large collection of tsam masks, used in Buddhist rituals, and intricate paintings and designs of Mongolian nomads. The Museum of Natural History is a treasure trove of ancient history, with displays of fossils, geological finds, and native plants and animals. The National Museum of Mongolia includes ancient art and tools, traditional costumes, jewelry, hats, blankets, and carpets. An entire floor contains exhibits on the Mongol Empire, complete with armor, swords, saddles, bows and arrows, and official documents. Several temples and historic sites in Ulaanbaatar have been restored and are now museums, including the Choijin Lama Temple and the last great khan's winter palace.

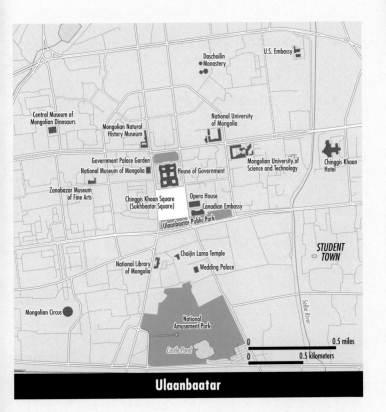

Ulaanbaatar

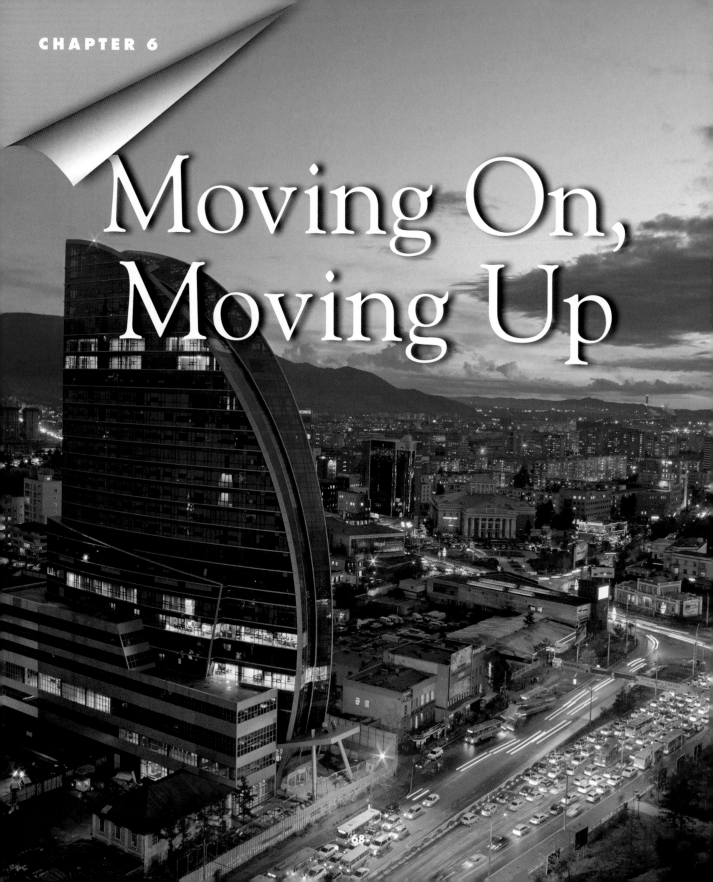

CHAPTER 6

Moving On, Moving Up

M ONGOLIA, LONG ISOLATED FROM MUCH OF the rest of the world, has a rapidly growing economy today. The country is rich in minerals and is experiencing a boom in tourism. Still, in many parts of the country, people continue to live traditional lives, herding and farming. But as new skyscrapers rise above historic buildings in Ulaanbaatar, a feeling of excitement and change fills the nation.

Opposite: **Many skyscrapers have risen in Ulaanbaatar. The tallest is the Blue Sky Tower, a twenty-five-story hotel and office building completed in 2009.**

Staying with Tradition

Mongolians have always been strong and self-sufficient. Being a traditional nomadic people living in a vast and often harsh land, success on their terms has required determination and hard physical labor. After the Soviet departure from Mongolia in 1990, many city and town dwellers returned to traditional ways of earning a living, including nomadic herding and farming. Today, nearly one-third of Mongolians are employed in livestock and agriculture. Only 1 percent of the land is arable, or fertile enough to support crops. The main crops grown are wheat, barley, potatoes, cabbage, and carrots. Fruits in Mongolia are primarily limited to berries and melons. Most Mongolian agriculture workers raise livestock. Some raise animals on privately owned land, but many follow tradition as nomadic herders. Herders generally set up four camps a year. Their locations depend on the weather and the availability of good pastureland.

A farmer checks on the wheat in his field. Wheat is the most common crop grown in Mongolia.

There are more than 45 million livestock animals in Mongolia. The main animals raised are the "five snouts": horses, cows, sheep, camels, and goats. Horses are raised for transportation, meat, and milk. Cows are raised for meat, leather, and milk, which is used to make yogurt and cheese. Sheep are the herders' most useful animals, raised for meat, milk, wool that is made into clothing and blankets, and hides that are used to cover gers. Bactrian camels are also raised for meat, milk, and wool, and they are used as pack animals when the herding groups move from one place to the next.

Kashmir goats are the second most popular livestock animals after sheep. They are raised for their meat, milk, and their especially soft wool, called cashmere. Mongolia exports some of the highest quality cashmere in the world and is the second largest producer of cashmere after China. Kashmir goats are a herder's best income-producing animals. A herder

Many Mongolian herders use a traditional lasso called an uurga, which consists of a long pole with a loop of rope on the end.

might make about US$16 for 1 pound (0.5 kg) of quality cashmere. Each goat sheds around 1 pound (0.5 kg) of cashmere wool each year. Goats are easy to raise. They will eat practically any grass, and often have twins and triplets, so herds are usually quite large. A successful herding family might have as many as two thousand goats.

Natural Resources

Both Russia and China have invested heavily in mining in Mongolia. This investment has led to an increase in jobs. Many young people are rejecting herding as a livelihood because mining pays better. Towns and cities near mines are also booming, providing jobs for construction and service workers.

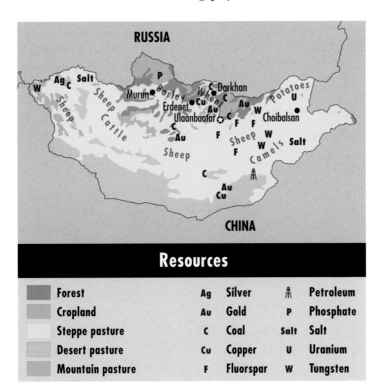

The largest gold and copper mine in Mongolia, and one of the largest in the world, is the Oyu Tolgoi mine in the Gobi Desert. It produces 970,000,000 pounds (440,000 metric tons) of copper each year and 330,000 ounces (9,355 kg) of gold. The mine employs sixteen thousand miners.

Mongolia also mines silver and is estimated to have 162 billion tons of coal in the ground. China imports most of

Mongolia's coal. The largest mine is a massive open-pit mine in the Gobi Desert not far from the Chinese border. Over remote desert roads, large trucks haul 240 tons of coal at a time to their destinations.

Workers excavate at the Oyu Tolgoi copper mine.

Manufacturing

During the years when Mongolia was under Soviet control, it manufactured far more goods than it does today, producing paper, soap, textiles, furniture, blankets, food products, leather goods, and other products. During that time, almost one-third of the country's economy was based on manufacturing. Today, manufacturing makes up less than 10 percent of the Mongolian economy.

But Mongolia is becoming wealthier, and customers are demanding more and better products. Mongolian manufacturers are trying to meet the demand for food products,

What Mongolia Grows, Makes, and Mines

AGRICULTURE (2013)

Wheat	387,000 metric tons
Sheep	20,600,000 animals
Goats	19,218,500 animals

MANUFACTURING

Food processing (2014)	US$11.6 million USD
Beverages (2012)	US$60 million USD
Wool carpets	710,000 square meters

MINING

Hard coal (2011)	26,800,000 metric tons
Iron ore (2012)	7,561,400 metric tons
Copper (2012)	347,600 metric tons

beverages, electronics, and clothing. Mongolians continue to produce traditional items such as leather goods, textiles, camel-hair blankets, and cashmere. But Mongolian factories are also turning raw materials into higher-priced finished goods for export. These goods include cashmere clothing, furniture, copper wiring, and steel building materials.

Services

Service jobs make up about 50 percent of the economy. Services are jobs people do for one another, such as jobs in health care, tourism, banking, education, retail sales, construction, trucking, and government. Many service industries are growing in Mongolia, particularly in mining regions.

Tourism is also expanding in Mongolia. For mountain climbers, bird-watchers, ancient-history buffs, and others, Mongolia offers exciting discoveries. It is a new tourist destination. However, since Mongolia has limited transportation options and accommodations, the industry is still developing. Ulaanbaatar has modern hotels, museums, and restaurants. In other parts of the country, visitors are more likely to experience "homestays," where they sleep in a ger, drink fermented mare's milk tea, and take a camel ride.

Workers run sewing machines at a cashmere factory in Ulaanbaatar.

Money Facts

The currency of Mongolia is the tugrik. Bills come in denominations of 5, 10, 20, 50, 100, 500, 1,000, 5,000, 10,000, and 20,000 tugriks. Each denomination has a different predominant color. The 20,000-tugrik note, for example, is orange and bears the likeness of Chinggis Khan. Sukhbaatar, a hero who helped force the Chinese out of Mongolia, appears on the 10, 50, and 100 tugrik notes. Next to his image is the golden soyombo, the national symbol of Mongolia. The 1,000-tugrik note bears an image of Chinggis Khan's ger, which was so large that it had to be transported by a team of oxen. In 2015, US$1.00 equaled 1,993 tugriks.

A Mongolian doctor examines a child. Mongolia has 2.84 doctors for every 1,000 people. The United States, in comparison, has 2.45 doctors per 1,000 people.

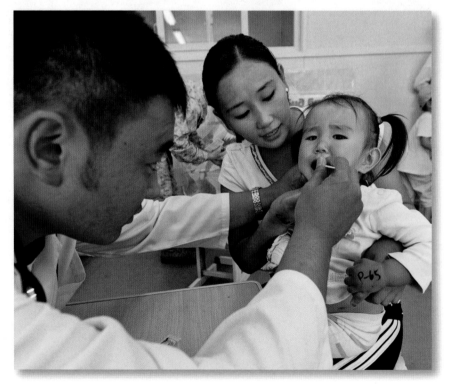

Transportation and Communications

The Soviet government put a priority on developing transportation in Mongolia, but when the Soviets left the country, the transportation system remained limited. To this day, there is only one major railroad line, the Trans-Mongolian Railway, which runs north and south between Russia and China. The country has just slightly more than 31,000 miles (50,000 km) of highway. Most of the roads connect Ulaanbaatar and regional centers, but only 1,250 miles (2,000 km) of them are paved. The rest are gravel or earthen. Relatively few people own cars, except in Ulaanbaatar, where traffic jams are common. Many people share rides in taxis, cars, and vans and it is not an unusual sight at all to see camels and yaks carrying cargo through the main streets of town.

The Trans-Mongolian Railway carries passengers across the vast Mongolian steppe.

It is also not unusual to see a person riding a camel and talking on a cell phone. More than three million cell phones are in use in Mongolia, which is slightly more than there are citizens. Less than 20 percent of the population used the Internet in 2014, but that is increasing.

Energy

Mongolia has an abundance of coal, and coal-fired power plants provide most of the country's electricity. The country also imports natural gas from Russia as well as oil for vehicles. Given that winters are long and cold, Mongolians require enormous amounts of electricity to heat their homes. When electricity needs are at their height, Ulaanbaatar burns so much wood and coal that in winter, it has become the second most polluted city in the world.

Elsewhere, the country is known for its sunny skies and powerful winds. This has made the country ripe for investment in solar and wind power. A new government program gives portable solar panels to nomadic herders who install them outside their gers. Environmentalists are also seeking ways to curb Ulaanbaatar's smog, which chokes the winter skies.

Many gers now use solar panels to provide electricity.

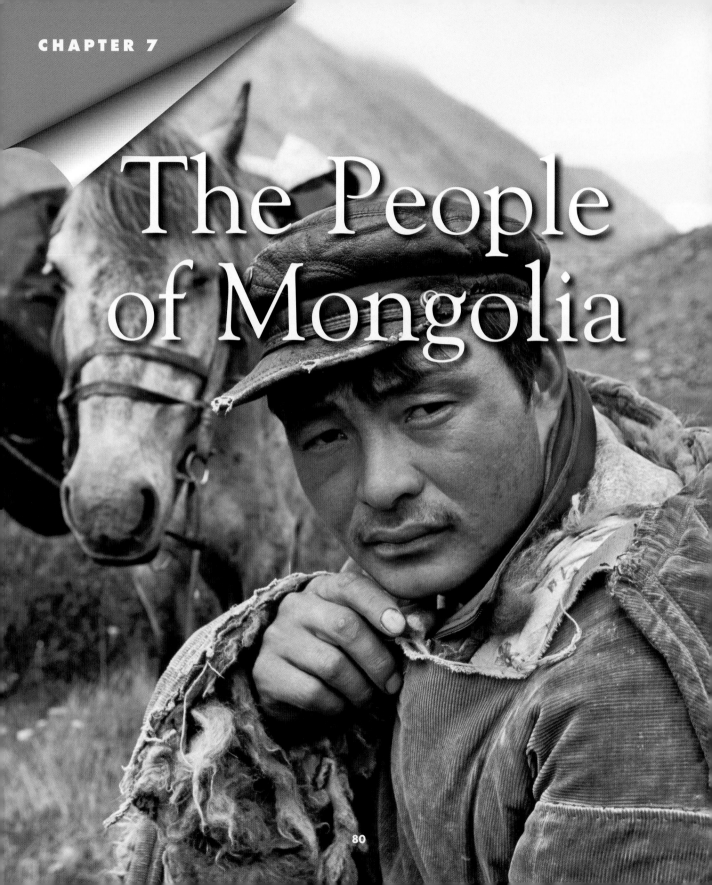

CHAPTER 7

The People of Mongolia

MONGOLIA IS HOME TO MANY DIFFERENT groups and clans. In ancient times, the groups sometimes raided one another. Rival groups were united, however, by Chinggis Khan and remained so during the Mongol Empire. Conflicts again arose after the empire broke apart. But, today, the rivalries have disappeared, even as people remain loyal to the heritage of their individual group and clan. Most major cultural differences between the groups have also faded, although a few groups retain unique cultures.

Ethnic Groups

More than 90 percent of Mongolians belong to the Mongolian ethnic group. Within this group, there are about twenty extended family groups, sometimes called tribes. The Khalkhas are the largest group of ethnic Mongolians. They are said to be direct descendants of Chinggis Khan. The Khalkha dialact, or version, of Mongolian is spoken by most people in the country.

Population by Ethnic Groups in Mongolia (2010)	
Khalkha	2,168,141
Kazakh	101,526
Dorvod	72,403
Bayad	56,573
Buryat	45,087
Zakhchin	32,845
Dariganga	27,412
Uriankhai	26,654
Darkhad	21,558
Khotogoid	15,460
Torguud	14,176
Khoton	11,304
Myangad	6,592
Barga	2,989
Uzemchin	2,577
Tsaatan	282
Other	3,447

The Kazakh people are the second-largest ethnic group in Mongolia, and the largest group that is not ethnically Mongolian. About one hundred thousand Kazakhs live in Mongolia, most in the far western part of the country, high in the mountains of the Altai range and nearby plains. The Kazakhs, who are Muslim, speak their own language, which is similar to Turkish.

The Dorvod group lives mainly in western Mongolia. In the seventeenth century, part of the clan split off from the main group and settled near Russia. During the Soviet

Some people in northern Mongolia live in cone-shaped tents, rather than in gers.

era, many of the clan wanted to secede from Mongolia and become part of Russia. The Bayad people live mainly in the north-central river valleys.

About 500,000 Buryat people live on the Siberian plateau, but less than 50,000 live in Mongolia. The Mongolian Buryat people share many customs with their Russian relatives, such as living in Russian-style wooden houses instead of gers. They also have their own language and their own script. A smaller ethnic Mongolian subgroup is the Tsaatan, who live in the northwest. They are sometimes called the reindeer people because their livelihoods are centered on herding reindeer.

The Tsaatan people keep reindeer for their milk. They also ride the reindeer and use them as pack animals.

Naming Names

During the communist era, Mongolians lost more than personal freedoms and private property; they also lost their names. Traditionally, Mongolians used a given name and a clan name. But the Soviet government was concerned that people would be more loyal to their clans than to the central government. So in 1925 they outlawed the use of clan names, leaving Mongolians with just a first name. To distinguish themselves from one another some Mongolians added their father's name or an initial to their first name. But confusion still reigned.

After the Soviets left Mongolia, the Great Khural reinstituted the use of clan names. Most people had long forgotten their clan name, however. To rediscover these names, researchers helped people interview elderly villagers, and everyone pored over family documents, historical records, and birth, death, and marriage records. Some people opted to make up a name, or take a name from a place, an animal, or someone they admired. A Mongolian astronaut took the name "Cosmos." Popular new names included "Eagle," "Wolf," and "Hunter." So many people wanted to name themselves after Chinggis Khan's clan name, Borjigin, that the government put a stop to it. It is estimated that nearly 50 percent of Mongolians do not know their true clan name, but today, Mongolians once again carry identification cards showing a first and last name.

The Uriankhai people live in western Mongolia near the Kazakhs. The Tuvans are a clan within the Uriankhai ethnic group who have their own language. They are known around the world for throat singing, an unusual style of singing in which one person can produce three notes at one time.

During the thirteenth century, many western Mongolian ethnic groups battled eastern groups, which were led by Chinggis Khan. The western groups were known as the Four Allies, and they spoke a language called Oirat, meaning "ally." The Zakhchin people who live in the western mountains still speak the Oirat language. Their name means "border people." Other Oirat speakers include the Khoton and the Myangad people.

Groups living in eastern Mongolia include the nomadic Dariganga, whose traditional home is the high volcanic region near the Gobi Desert, the Barga, the Uzemchin, and the Khamnigan.

Languages

Mongolian, the official language of Mongolia, is spoken by 90 percent of the population. In the western part of the country, Kazakh, Tuvan, and Oirat are also spoken. The Buryat people also have their own language. Programs in schools teach children their ethnic heritage language. In 2014, a program began for Tuvan students, who received newly printed books written in a new Tuvan-Mongolian alphabet. Previously, the language and culture had been passed down through handwritten texts from the Republic of Tuva in Russia. Those books did not accurately reflect the dialects, alphabet, and culture of the Tuvan people in Mongolia.

Two Tuvan men play a game of chess.

Speaking Mongolian

Sain baina uu?	Hello.
Bayartai.	Good-bye.
Ta sain suuj baina uu?	How are you?
Bi sain. Ta sain uu?	I am fine. How are you?
Mash ikh bayarlalaa.	Thank you very much.
Zugeer zugeer.	You're welcome.

Tourists enjoy a camel ride in the Gobi Desert. More than four hundred thousand foreign visitors travel to Mongolia each year.

In addition to the speakers of the various heritage languages in Mongolia, native speakers of Russian, Chinese, Uighur, and Korean also live there. Today, an increasing number of Mongolians speak English. This is especially true of people who hold professional jobs or work in the tourist industry.

Mongolian is written using a variety of alphabets. Beginning in 1941, a time when the Soviet Union dominated Mongolia, Mongolia officially adopted the Cyrillic alphabet that was used there. Today, books, newspapers, and magazines are still written in Cyrillic. But because Cyrillic is less common on the Internet than some other writing systems, many Mongolians are now using the Latin alphabet, the alphabet used to write English.

Many signs in Mongolia are written in the Cyrillic alphabet.

Education

Traditionally, many children of nomad families helped with herding and were unable to go to school. During Soviet rule, new schools were established, and children were taught to write in Cyrillic. When the Soviets left Mongolia, it was up to the new Mongolian government to continue the progress.

They built more rural schools as well as boarding schools to educate children while their parents are herding. Because of the rapid increase in population in Ulaanbaatar, many new schools are also being built there.

Today, children are required to attend school from ages six to fifteen. They may choose to attend another two years of high school to study a trade or prepare to attend a college or university. Some of the top universities in Mongolia are the National University, Mongolian University of Science and Technology, and Mongolian State University of Agriculture.

In the City

Mongolia is one of the world's least densely populated countries. Across the country as a whole, an average of just 5 people live in every square mile (1.9 people per sq km). Cities are few. The largest city is the capital, Ulaanbaatar, where nearly half of all Mongolians live.

Many of the country's earliest cities were nomadic camps or settlements established along trade routes between China and Europe. Later cities evolved around Buddhist monasteries. But in the 1930s, the government of the Soviet Union controlled Mongolia. Officials banished the monasteries and so weakened the communities built around them. The Soviets built new factories, and the new cities that were created reflected Soviet ideas and design. Cities such as Erdenet and Darkhan were built by the Soviets. Today, about seven out of every ten Mongolians live in cities.

Population of Major Cities (2013 est.)	
Ulaanbaatar	1,226,991
Erdenet	83,379
Darkhan	74,738
Choibalsan	38,537
Murun	35,789

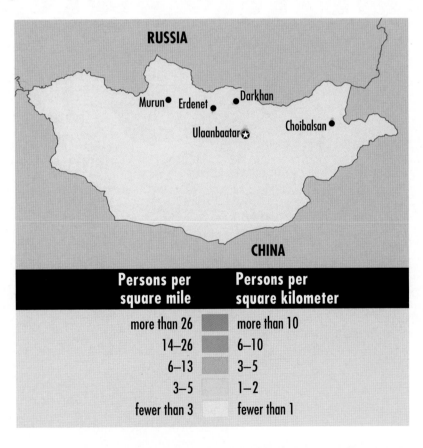

Persons per square mile		Persons per square kilometer
more than 26		more than 10
14–26		6–10
6–13		3–5
3–5		1–2
fewer than 3		fewer than 1

CHAPTER 8

Eternal Blue Heaven

AS PEOPLE MIGRATED TO MONGOLIA FROM MANY lands, they brought their religions with them. The new faiths became intermingled with the ancient beliefs of the Mongolian people. Some of these religions faded away, while others flourished.

Faith of the Ancients

Ancient people of Mongolia worshipped trees, rocks, lakes, rivers, and animals. Thousands of years ago, nomadic people left behind stone totems throughout the steppe. They erected hundreds of these upright stone slabs, 3 to 12 feet high (1 to 4 m). The stones were carved with graceful images of deer and other animals galloping toward the sun. Often called deer stones, these totems are some of the most important archaeological treasures of central Asia.

Religion in Mongolia (2010)	
Buddhist	53%
Muslim	3%
Christian	2%
Shamanist	3%
None	39%

Ancient stories tell of the rise of the Mongol people. According to these stories, the ancestors of the Mongolians are the Blue Wolf and the Fallow Doe. These are two very different beings, one the hunter and one the hunted. Yet it was their destiny to rebuild the world, and they realized that they needed each other to survive. The Blue Wolf brought courage and strength to their union. The Fallow Doe brought gentleness, intuition, and elegance. Together, they gave birth to the Mongol people.

Large rock burial grounds also remain in Mongolia. Later groups adopted the deer and other totem animals as their own, and these creatures became important in Mongolian mythology.

Later nomadic groups worshipped a supreme god known as Tengri, meaning Eternal Blue Heaven, or Father Sky, and his companion, Eje, or Mother Earth. Historical accounts show that Chinggis Khan believed Tengri was on his side. Whenever he rode into battle, he cried, "By the will of the Eternal Blue Heaven."

Tengri is said to have a son, Gesar, who was sent to earth as a shaman, or holy man, to heal the world. He is celebrated today in a festival lasting several days. Followers of the religion known as Tengriism place offerings at mountaintop sites. The offering may be small rocks or more valuable objects such as money, candies, cakes, bowls of milk, and prized household belongings. The most visually striking offerings are beautiful blue scarves, known as *khadags*, worn by women.

Shamanism

Traditionally, Mongolia's nomads believed that the natural world was sacred and that spirits existed around them. Most of the time, nomads were able to tackle their own misfor-

Blue scarves are tied to a statue of a Tengri shaman.

tunes such as illnesses. They made offerings, obeyed rules of conduct, consumed natural plant medicines, and performed healing dances and rituals. But when hardships got too great, people sought out a shaman, who could guide them in and

A Mongolian shaman performs a ceremony. Both men and women can be shamans.

protect them from the spirit world. Shamanism is still practiced in many, mostly rural, communities in Mongolia.

Shamans are believed to have a deep knowledge of the healing properties of plants. They perform rituals by singing, chanting, dancing, and drumming to summon the spirits. Shamans wear special costumes and masks. They also wear a mirror on the chest to deflect the advances of evil spirits. They sometimes use other tools such as staffs topped with carved horse heads to lead them on spirit journeys, and special fans to wave evil spirits away from the sick. Besides healing the sick, shamans are called upon to make rain, to lure animals into hunting grounds, or to improve a family's luck.

If a task is particularly difficult, the shaman will go into a trance. It is said that in this state, the shaman has entered the depths of the spirit world. Other people participate in the ritual by chanting and drumming in hopes that the shaman will return successful and unscathed.

The Buddha Speaks

The most common religion in Mongolia today came to the region through war. During the thirteenth century, Mongolia's many religions coexisted, even though many groups were constantly at war. Under Chinggis Khan, who himself was tolerant of all religions, the Mongol army defeated nearby Tibet. Through this, Tibetan Buddhism came to Mongolia.

Buddhism began in India more than 2,500 years ago, when a wealthy prince saw a world of suffering around him. He left his palace and family and wandered, seeking peace and calm in the face of suffering and death. He nearly despaired, until one day he awoke from sleeping under a tree and saw a way to find peace and joy. He took the name Buddha, which means the Enlightened

Young monks have a meal at a monastery in Mongolia.

A giant Buddha statue in Darkhan

One. Buddha explained what are known as the Four Noble Truths: Life is filled with suffering; suffering is caused by people's wants; suffering can end when people stop wanting things, such as more pleasure and more power; and to stop wanting things, people must follow basic rules called the Eightfold Path. These rules ask people to do their best by being truthful, kind, respectful, thoughtful, careful, and by resisting evil.

Creator of the Script

In 1244, Phagpa (below), the ten-year-old nephew of a renowned Tibetan lama, took religious vows to become a Buddhist monk. The boy was so clever that he was able to assist his uncle in transcribing Buddhist scriptures into Mongolian. In 1253, Kublai Khan (right) called the young man to his court in China. The great khan was impressed with Phagpa and asked him to remain at the palace and provide religious instruction. The young lama agreed but informed the great khan that he must bow before him whenever they met to show respect for his religious authority. Phagpa required that

his royal student sit at a height below him, and when traveling, be behind him. But Kublai Khan protested these demands, saying that his supreme power would be put into question. They finally agreed that the great khan would bow before the young lama and sit lower than him, but only in private.

Phagpa became politically powerful in the khan's court and within Buddhism. In 1265, he returned to Tibet, where he encouraged different Buddhist groups to unify under one government. When Phagpa returned to China, he presented Kublai Khan with a specialized script to use for official documents that could be read in both Chinese and Mongolian. Kublai Khan was so pleased he gave Phagpa the titles Miraculous Divine Lord Under the Sky and Above the Earth, Creator of the Script, Messenger of Peace throughout the World, and Possessor of the Five Higher Sciences.

Sacred Sites

The grandest Buddhist temples contain paintings, sculptures, ornate prayer wheels (right), and golden stupas. A stupa is a large domed structure built on top of something sacred, such as the bones of a renowned lama, a special scripture, or a selection of mantras. A mantra is a word, sound, or phrase that can be used to send out blessings and healing energy. Some of the largest prayer wheels contain as many as a million mantras written inside. A person spins the prayer wheel clockwise and chants a mantra. This is said to release into the world all of the mantras inside the wheel.

In the 1500s, Altan Khan was sent to Tibet where he met a Buddhist priest, or lama, named Sakya Pandita. Altan Khan converted to Buddhism. Sakya's nephew, also a lama, went to the court of Kublai Khan, where he was held in high esteem. Although the lama converted many nobles to Buddhism, the lama had really been sent to retain friendly relations between Mongolia and Tibet. In Tibet, Altan Khan called the highest-ranking Buddhist lama the Dalai Lama, meaning "one whose wisdom is as deep as the ocean." The influence of these men helped spread the teachings of the Buddha. Many Tibetan lamas came to Mongolia to convince people to give up their religions, especially Shamanism.

When Buddhist lamas arrived in Mongolia, they realized that to attract people to Buddhism, they needed to link their faith to those of the Mongolian people. The lamas built their monasteries near sacred locations. Both Buddhism and Shamanism incorporated drumming, chanting, and dancing in their rituals. Lamas and shamans both wore costumes during special rituals. Lamas carried symbolic swords decorated with a horse's head, similar to the decorated staffs sometimes carried by shamans. By the end of the nineteenth century, Mongolia had more than 580 Buddhist monasteries and temples, and most Mongolians were Buddhist. The largest group that did not become Buddhist was the Kazakhs of western Mongolia, who practice Islam.

Most ethnic Kazakhs are Muslim. In the Bayan-Ölgii region of western Mongolia, nearly 90 percent of the population is Muslim.

Erdene-Dzuu

The oldest temple to have partially escaped the wrath of the communists is Erdene-Dzuu, a temple complex built atop the ruins of a palace of a son of Chinggis Khan. The center of a thriving empire, the palace had silver fountains and ornate decorations made from gold, silver, and rare gems. The palace had been destroyed in battle, but in the sixteenth century, lamas cleared away the rubble and used the debris to build a massive walled complex. The complex contained seventy temples, hundreds of shrines and monuments, and 108 stupas (108 is a holy number in Buddhism), each holding a sacred object or scripture. At one time, more than two thousand lamas lived at Erdene-Dzuu. During communist times, most of the temples were destroyed, and the lamas were imprisoned or killed. The monastery was shut down, and only fourteen temples and shrines in the complex were left standing. Today, the buildings are a museum. Some visitors say that the temple brings more sadness than joy as they reflect on the destruction of so much beauty, history, and goodness.

Destruction and Recovery

The Soviet government believed that in order for people to modernize, they needed to do away with religion. When the communists took over Mongolia, they went on a rampage against Buddhism. At the time, Mongolia had more than seven hundred temples and thousands of monasteries, schools, shrines, and monuments. The Buddhist church was quite wealthy. Between the 1930s and the 1960s, the communists took power and property away from the Buddhists and tried to turn Mongolia into an atheist society, one that followed no religion. The government shut religious schools and monasteries, razed more than six hundred temples, and murdered, banished, or imprisoned thousands of lamas. By the time communists left in 1990, few temples still stood and few lamas remained to teach the faithful.

In 1990, freedom of religion was restored. Lamas returned to rebuild their monasteries and temples. But the long period without religion had changed people's habits. At one time, 90 percent of Mongolians were Buddhist; today, about 50 percent are Buddhist. Nearly four out of ten say they no longer practice any religion.

Buddhist Holidays

Mongolians celebrate two major Buddhist holidays. Ikh Duichen celebrates Buddha's three life changes—his birth, the day he became awakened, and the day he reached nirvana, which is a state of eternal peace and understanding. The holiday usually falls in early summer. In Ulaanbaatar, the day is celebrated with lavish street decorations, parades, music, and the *tsam* dance. Tsam dancers (left) wear large, elaborate, and often frightening masks. Their dramatic movements are meant to ward off evil.

Mongolians celebrate Baljinnyam and Dashnyam, two Buddhist deities, on a day in early autumn. There is no single way that Mongolians honor the day. People believe that the day brings all manner of good things, such as happiness and wealth. Because of this, Mongolians often do notable things on this day, such as get married, start a new business, move to a new house, or set out on a journey. Many people, however, simply gather with friends and family and enjoy a lively meal.

CHAPTER 9

Rhythm of Life

MUSIC IS VERY MUCH A PART OF MONGOLIAN
life. One of the oldest forms of music is the long song, based
on epic poetry. The music often sounds sad and brings to mind
the solitude of the herders' lives on the vast steppe. A sole
singer performs the long song, holding a note for as long as
possible. Sometimes a fiddle or lute accompanies the singer.
A newer form of music is the short song, which is livelier and
uses more instruments. The short song touches on popular
themes such as love, home, and horses. Short songs are a part
of most social events today.

Musical Traditions

The Tuva people are renowned for an unusual ancient musical
tradition called *khoomii*, or throat singing. This art is performed by a solo singer who can sing three notes at the same
time. The sounds are eerie and powerful. They often imitate

Opposite: **A woman plays
a horsehead fiddle, the
national instrument of
Mongolia.**

A throat singer performs in Ulaanbaatar.

sounds from nature such as birdcalls, the wind, or rushing rivers. Throat singing is usually performed by men. Boys begin training at a young age. Today, some girls are learning the art.

Mongolian musicians in ancient times created a unique instrument called a horsehead fiddle. The fiddle is a trapezoid, a four-sided shape with two sides that are parallel and two sides that are not parallel. It has two long horsehair strings and is played using a horsehair bow. Usually a horse's head is carved onto the top of the fiddle. Early Mongolian musicians also invented a mouth harp made of leather, bamboo, or iron. Most often, it is played by a shaman. Mongolian musicians today also make and play four-string fiddles, lutes, flutes, and a zither that has fourteen silk strings.

Brush and Needle

Throughout history, Mongolian painters have used a variety of materials to create their art, including silk, leather hides, felt, cotton, and linen. Traditionally, they made their paints from Mongolia's mineral-rich environment, using metals such as gold, silver, copper, and iron. They mixed these ingredients, as well as pearls and coral shells from China, with ground-up animal bones and horns boiled in sweet syrup. To create a more meaningful paint, artists also mixed in earth or water from sacred sites.

Many gers have brightly painted doors. The doors often feature traditional Buddhist symbols, such as a never-ending knot.

The earliest art in Mongolia was cave paintings. Embroidery is another ancient Mongolian art form. Nomadic craftspeople embellished wool felt to decorate their carpets, blankets, and the walls of their gers. Nomads crafted detailed paintings on small pieces of fabric, in a style known as *zurag*, that could be transported easily. Mongolians created symbols and geometric designs inspired by nature, plants, and animal forms. One of the best-known symbols is the *olzii*, or never-ending knot. The symbol represents the universe and is said to bring long life and happiness to the user.

Mongolian clothing is frequently decorated with brightly colored embroidery.

This thangka depicts a mountain god.

In the eighteenth century, Buddhist lamas learned to do appliqué and embroidery on silk and fine cloth, creating a prized religious art form called *thangka*. Widely used throughout the Buddhist world, a thangka depicts religious symbols and scenes and is stored rolled up like a scroll. Most thangkas are unrolled privately and used during meditation and prayer.

Architecture

Mongolian architecture has a long history. Archaeologists have unearthed burial monuments dating to the fourth century BCE. Beginning in the sixth century CE, the powerful Xiongnu group made portable tents on wheels and folding gers. The nobles lived in permanent buildings made of stone, and the village was protected by huge stone walls.

Mongolian nomads erecting a ger. It takes a Mongolian family between one and two hours to put up their ger.

A ger is made of folding lattice walls. Large spokes radiate out from the center of the roof to supporting poles. The walls and roof are covered in brightly colored and decorated felt and cloth that are fastened to the poles with horsehair ropes. An opening acts as a door and a small hole in the upper part of the ger vents smoke from the cookstove. A ger camp is arranged in a circle, with the village elder's ger in the center. Historically, the circle helped prevent attacks from raiders.

A major architectural change came in the 1500s and 1600s, with the arrival of Buddhist lamas who built monasteries and temples in the Tibetan style, with features such as red tiered roofs. They were adorned with sculptures and stupas. Later, the temples included green Chinese tiles. In 1646, an artist named Zanabazar designed and built the first temple that combined Tibetan, Chinese, and round ger-style architecture.

Master of Arts

Zanabazar (below) is often considered the greatest Mongolian artist. Born in 1635 into a noble Khalkha family, his talents were recognized at an early age. Sent to a monastery school in Tibet, he developed many skills. By age fifteen, he had become a lama. His name means "brilliant child."

After returning to Mongolia, he created detailed bronze sculptures of Buddhist deities (right). He also mastered the art of Buddhist appliqué and embroidery as well as jewelry making and sculpting in wood and stone. He developed the Soyombo script used by the ruling khans for official documents, as well as the official symbol of Mongolia, the golden soyombo.

Zanabazar turned to architecture as another means of artistic expression. He designed and oversaw the construction of many temples, developing a unique style that combined Tibetan architecture with the Mongolian ger. His Batu-Tsagaan Tsogchin temple in Urga influenced many future architects. The temple's large, circular, domed-shaped structure was supported by 108 columns, the Buddhist holy number. For all his achievements, he was anointed a Living Buddha, one of the highest honors in Buddhism. Today, visitors to Ulaanbaatar can view many of his works at the Zanabazar Museum of Fine Arts.

The next large major influence on Mongolian architecture came from Russians. Their early buildings were made of logs and many places of worship had domed roofs. In the early 1900s, Russians built in a style that included columns, arches, and half-dome shapes. Many of Ulaanbaatar's official buildings are in this style, including the House of Government, the Opera House, the State Library, and the Zanabazar Museum. Later, the communist government destroyed hundreds of temples, monasteries, and historic buildings, wiping out centuries of unique architecture. Then the government erected rows

The Mongolian State Academic Theater of Opera and Ballet sits on Sukhbaatar Square. The Soviets built it in a neoclassical style, with columns that recall ancient Greece.

The Weeping Camel

Byambasuren Davaa is one of Mongolia's most successful filmmakers. Born in Ulaanbaatar in 1971, she studied filmmaking at the Movie Academy in Ulaanbaatar and later worked for Mongolian National Television. Her first movie, called *The Story of the Weeping Camel*, was nominated for an Academy Award for Best Documentary film. The movie, which she wrote and produced, follows a herding family in the Gobi Desert. One of their camels rejects her newborn calf so the family seeks out a group of lamas to perform a ritual. The lamas fail to convince the mother

THE STORY of the WEEPING CAMEL

BYAMBASUREN DAVAA & LUIGI FALORNI

to accept the calf, so the family sends a boy to a distant village to seek help. He returns with a musician who plays the horsehead fiddle. With the herders sitting in a circle around the camel and her calf, the musician plays and a woman sings a traditional song. Its eerie beauty brings the camel to tears and she unites with her calf. Byambasuren Davaa used local herders as well as professional actors in her film. She was one of the first people to show the outside world the true lifestyle of nomadic herders in the Gobi Desert. She has since made other highly acclaimed films about Mongolia—*The Cave of the Yellow Dog* and *The Two Horses of Genghis Khan*.

Concrete apartment buildings from the Soviet era line the streets of Erdenet.

and rows of tall concrete buildings in Ulaanbaatar and other cities. After the Soviets departed, many Mongolians, including those of little means, contributed money to rebuild and restore what remained of the temples and monasteries.

Telling the Story

Mongolia's oldest stories were not written down. Instead, they were passed down orally through the generations. The first written literature in Mongolia was epic poetry. The earliest and best-known text is the *The Secret History of the Mongols*, which tells the story of Chinggis Khan. *The Epic of King Geser* is a popular story cycle that tells of a fearless king who battled monsters in an imaginary land. Mongolians remain fond of epic poetry and often listen to readings on the radio or online.

Some modern Mongolian writers have made a name for themselves. In the early twentieth century, author, poet, and playwright Dashdorjiin Natsagdorj founded the Mongolian Writer's Union. He was noted for his novels, *Three Fateful Hills* and *The Lama's Tears*. The communist government imprisoned him in the 1930s when he wrote patriotic verses about revolution and freedom. Other writers also were detained and not allowed to publish their works. After 1990, writers were once again free to express themselves. Two well-known authors, Lodongiin Tüdew and Oeled Chahar Ligden, compiled anthologies of previously banned Mongolian stories and plays. David Kugultinov, who had been a political prisoner, became well known in Mongolia and beyond for his poetry.

David Kugultinov published his first book of poetry at age eighteen. Just a few years later he was arrested, however, and he spent more than ten years as a political prisoner before emerging to become a prominent poet.

CHAPTER 10

Ride in Peace

MONGOLIA IS AN ANCIENT LAND WITH A RICH history, but in some ways the country is quite young. For example, the people have had democracy for just a few decades. Also, the population is young, with nearly half of Mongolians under the age of thirty. Mongolian society and government together are experiencing changes and mixing the treasured customs of the past with the promise of the future.

Opposite: **Although many Mongolians still ride horses across the steppe, motorcycles are also common.**

Family Life

Families in Mongolia are traditionally close. Nomads, for example, share strong bonds because they live and travel together with their herds. Though nomads may not mix much with other groups, they are hospitable to guests. In the past, families had many children, but in recent years, both urban and rural families are having fewer children. The average Mongolian family now has two or three children.

The Hair Cut

An important ceremony in the lives of children is called Daah Urgeeh, or the hair-cutting ceremony. For the first three to six years of life, Mongolian parents let their child's hair grow. Children are precious in Mongolian society, and parents carry a deep fear that their child may not survive their early years. Mongolians celebrate when the child grows beyond babyhood. The Daah Urgeeh is held on an auspicious date when a boy is three or five and when a girl is four or six. Family and friends come to the child's home, and each person takes a turn cutting locks of hair. Guests bring gifts for the child—often money, a toy, or a blessing. After the ceremony, the hair is wrapped and stored in a blue khadag scarf and feasting begins.

Housing

In 2010, about 45 percent of Mongolians lived in gers. But not all people who live in gers live in rural areas. Nearly 30 percent of people who live within city limits live in gers.

Many people who made money in mining are moving to cities, particularly to Ulaanbaatar. New house and apartment construction is constant, and the city is filled with the sound of saws and the sight of construction cranes. Many rural people are also moving to cities, especially after the brutal winter of 2010 that killed millions of herd animals. They cannot afford the cost of housing in the city so they bring their gers with them. Huge, fenced-off communities of gers called *khashas* surround Ulaanbaatar. The khashas have little running water, prompting concern about the health of the residents. Also, rather than

At the Wedding Palace

Weddings traditionally take place on a day believed to bring good luck and happiness. Many Mongolians marry on the highly auspicious Baljinnyam and Dashnyam holiday.

In many traditional weddings, before the date is set, the groom's family brings gifts to the bride's family. In rural communities, livestock is a welcome gift. The bride's father also receives a pot of glue signifying the strength of the future union. Although families used to decide whom their children would marry, since the late twentieth century, people choose their own marriage partner.

Many preparations are required for a traditional nomad wedding (right). For example, the groom and his parents must craft the couple's new ger. The groom is responsible for lining the walls with felt and providing wood furniture. The bride buys pots and dishes and prepares the stove for cooking. On the day of the wedding, the groom and a village elder arrive at the bride's door. The door is locked and the groom must charm the family into opening the door. Once inside, he is given gifts

of food. The bride wears an elaborately embroidered silk or cotton tunic called a *del*. The groom also wears a del, but of a darker color. The bride leaves with the groom, followed by family and friends on horseback. A carpet is rolled out and everyone gathers around a table to sing, dance, tell jokes, eat, and drink. In villages, the feasting may go on for three to four days.

When city dwellers get married, the groom usually wears a suit and the bride wears a white embroidered gown and veil. Although Mongolian weddings now follow many Western customs, tradition still holds in some ways. After the service and before the reception, the bride sets a pyramid of sticks on fire to signify the purity of the marriage. During the reception, each table or group presents the couple with gifts, gives a toast, and sings a song. Many weddings in Ulaanbaatar are performed at the Wedding Palace (left), a large hall built by the Soviet government to direct marriages away from temples and other places of worship. On the Baljinnyam and Dashnyam holiday, so many weddings are scheduled that each couple barely has thirty minutes to complete their ceremony.

Ride in Peace **117**

heating with electricity, the people in gers use stoves that burn wood and coal, causing stifling air pollution in the winter. The government is trying to build permanent housing for people in the khashas, but many there do not want to leave their gers.

Clothing

Traditional Mongolian clothing was made for nomadic life. Besides being suited to both extreme cold and summer heat, garments were also decorative. A traditional garment called a *del* is often worn. It is a long tunic tied at the waist. Some are worn for everyday work clothes, while others made of fine fabrics are worn on special occasions. Mongolians also have colorful and unique hats that are finely embellished. Some are bonnets, others are cone-shaped or broad-brimmed, and many are lined with fur. Many women, especially in the countryside, wear headscarves. In Mongolia, headscarves are blue, symbolizing the sky. City dwellers generally wear Western-style clothing, pants, shirts, and dresses, but most have a del in their closet to wear at special events.

Food

In Ulaanbaatar, restaurants and stores sell a wide variety of foods from many regions of the world. Rural people have fewer choices. They eat grains, breads, noodles, potatoes, cabbage, berries, and especially dairy products and meat. Dairy products such as thick cream, butter, and kefir (a thin yogurt) are everyday foods. *Aaruul* is a cheese that rural people dry on the tops of their gers and take with them while herding. Popular drinks include mare's milk, and a fermented milk called *airag*. The most common meats in Mongolia are mutton and beef. They are usually cooked with handmade noodles or used in soups and dumplings. Mongolian food is not spicy. Most meals are prepared with a wok or a griddle.

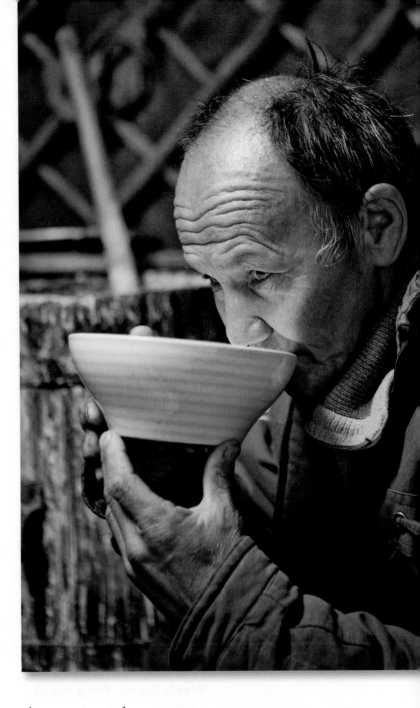

Mongolians always offer guests a bowl of airag.

Some foods are prepared only on special occasions. Mongolian barbeque is made for parties and festivals. Rather than cooking the meat from the outside, Mongolian barbeque

A boy plays basketball in a ger village in the Gobi Desert.

chefs place hot rocks inside the meat and cook it from the inside. On holidays, Mongolians make a special treat called *kheviin boov*, or "shoe sole cake." The cake is made in an oblong shape and filled with sweetened dried milk. Before baking, a special pattern carved from a wooden block is stamped onto the cake. Each family has its own individual stamp design. Some of the dough oozes to the sides, making the cake look like the sole of a shoe. Many of the cakes are served together on a platter. They are stacked to form a large tower.

Work Hard, Play Hard

Mongolians are passionate about sports. Traditional sports are wrestling, horse riding, falconry, and archery. People are also wild about basketball, volleyball, ice-skating, and soccer.

Mongolians even play soccer in the snow. During the long, cold winters, people stay inside and play chess, board and card games, Ping-Pong, and traditional games that use sheep anklebones for dice or tokens.

Mongolians also love to watch sports. During major sporting events, such as the Olympics and the World Cup soccer tournament, many Mongolians are glued to the televisions. Even herders on the steppe take time to sit in front of their solar-powered satellite TVs and cheer their favorite athletes. In international competitions, Mongolian athletes have won medals in judo, boxing, and sumo wrestling.

Playing with Shagai

Children play many different games using sheep anklebones, called *shagai*. Shagai can be thrown like dice, shot like marbles, or tossed in the air. In one popular game, children gather at least twenty shagai. They write the name of or draw one of four animals—horse, camel, goat, or sheep—on each of four sides of the bone. Each child keeps one shagai and the rest are tossed. The first player places his or her bone facing the tossed shagai. Then he or she flicks the shagai with middle finger and thumb toward a shagai showing the same animal on top. If the player succeeds in hitting the target without disturbing other shagai, then the player takes that piece and another turn. Play continues until all the pieces are gone, and the winner is the player with the most anklebones. Shagai are special, and most children keep theirs in pouches. They are also given as gifts to close friends.

Horse Riding

Horses are central to Mongolian culture. Horse culture is part of everyday life, even for people who live in cities. A common greeting is "Have you ridden well?" and a friendly way to say good-bye is "Ride in peace." In both cities and the country-side, children learn to ride at a young age.

Horse racing in Mongolia is a fiercely competitive sport. Races are not run on a circular track but rather in a straight line across the countryside. Mongolians also take part in trick riding

Children gallop across the grasslands in a horse race during the Naadam festival.

Mongolian wrestlers are some of the best in the world, and some of the best entertainers, too. The wrestlers, all large men, dress in bright red and blue costumes, consisting of a pair of tiny pants and shirts with no front or back, only sleeves that go across the shoulders and down the upper arm. The matches are held in a grassy field. The goal is to force the other player to touch a knee, elbow, or his back to the ground. Before the match, the competitors flap their arms up and down, squat, and slap their thighs in what is called the Eagle Dance. At the end of the match, they repeat the dance.

competitions, such as playing tug-of-war with an animal hide or picking a coin up off the ground while racing at a full gallop. Each year, the best riders compete in the Mongol Derby, a grueling 621-mile (1,000 km) race that follows the rugged course of Chinggis Khan's military communications route.

Archery and Falconry

The national sports of Mongolia come from its warrior and hunter past. During the days of the Mongol Empire, Mongolians were the finest archers in the world. Mongol archers could pull back a powerful bow and hit a target 400 feet (120 m) away, while standing in the stirrups of a galloping horse. The archer could also hit his target facing backward or hanging off of his saddle. Today's archery competitions are dramatic demonstrations of the archer's skill.

Mongolia's National Holidays

New Year's Day	January 1
Lunar New Year	February
International Women's Day	March 8
Mothers' and Children's Day	June 1
Naadam	July
Chinggis Khan's Birthday	November 14
Independence Day	December 29

Falconry, or hunting with eagles, is a sport that is thousands of years old. Mongolia is one of the few areas of the world where it is not only practiced as a sport, but is a means of livelihood. The Kazakh people of the Altai Mountains train eagles to hunt for them in the rough terrain of winter. The hunters, or falconers, release their eagles into the sky while they gallop on horseback over the steppe. The falconer and eagle communicate with each other with calls and whistles. When the eagle has successfully hunted a rabbit, fox, or wolf, the falconer retrieves the prey and the eagle returns home.

Time to Celebrate

Mongolians mark the passing of time with many different festivals. Naadam festivals are held in July throughout the country, but the largest one is in Ulaanbaatar. Naadam, meaning "festival of sports," is Mongolia's most popular festival. It dates back to the thirteenth century and celebrates the warrior skills of Chinggis Khan's army. The festival celebrates what are known as the Three Manly Arts: wrestling, horse racing, and archery.

The three-day festival in Ulaanbaatar opens with a parade led by riders wearing dels and colorful hats.

Singers and dancers perform the opening ceremony and then the games begin. The festival includes six types of horse racing competitions. Most of the jockeys are young, and most ride bareback so their horses are carrying the least weight possible. Blue silk ribbons are woven into the manes of the winners, an honor Chinggis Khan bestowed on his best horses. Hundreds of wrestlers compete in Ulaanbaatar's Naadam event. There are no weight classes, so wrestlers sometimes must compete against people twice their size. Recently, women have been allowed to compete in archery events. They shoot twenty arrows at a target 200 feet (60 m) away, and men shoot forty arrows at a target 250 feet (75 m) away. Throughout the festival, there are dance, music, and singing performances, as well as abundant food and drink.

Maidar Ergekh is a Buddhist holiday that celebrates the coming of Maidar, the Buddha of the

An archer takes aim during the Naadam festival in Ulaanbaatar.

Future. A statue of Maidar on a cart drawn by either a green wooden horse or a white elephant symbolizes the widespread success of Buddhism. During this festival, lamas lead a procession with the statue. They make their way through the crowd, extending blessings to the four directions and reading from sacred texts. Masked tsam dancers follow along until the statue is returned to its altar.

Mongolian lamas march through the street during the Maidar ceremony.

Tsagaan Sar is the celebration of the lunar New Year. Throughout the country, people attend Buddhist services, and many people, especially nomads, follow a wealth of rituals on this day. The celebration begins nearly a month before, when people thoroughly clean their gers. They must be finished cleaning by Bituun, the last day of the year. On that night, a huge meal is prepared and everyone must eat his or her fill in order to ensure good fortune and prosperity in the coming year. Before sunrise of the New Year, people leave their gers and bow to the four directions, while sprinkling milk to honor nature and the god Tengri. The day is filled with special greetings, gift giving, and visits to family, friends, and elders. At the day's end, everyone again gathers to play games, sing songs, and enjoy another feast, recalling the past and looking forward to a new year.

Young Mongolians relax together during Tsagaan Sar, the lunar new year.

Timeline

MONGOLIAN HISTORY

1911	The Qing dynasty falls and Outer Mongolia declares independence.
1919	The Chinese army occupies Outer Mongolia.
1920	The Mongolian People's Party is founded.
1921	Soviet troops drive China out of Mongolia.
1924	Mongolia renames itself the Mongolian People's Republic.
1936	The Soviet Union orders the destruction of Buddhist temples in Mongolia.
1989	Demonstrators in Sukhbaatar Square call for free elections and an end to Soviet control of Mongolia.
1990	The Soviet government withdraws from Mongolia.
1992	Mongolia changes its name back to Mongolia.
2010	Eight million livestock animals die in a zud.
2013	Oyu Tolgoi mine opens in the Gobi Desert.
2015	Mongolia becomes one of the fastest-growing economies in the world.

WORLD HISTORY

1789	The French Revolution begins.
1865	The American Civil War ends.
1879	The first practical lightbulb is invented.
1914	World War I begins.
1917	The Bolshevik Revolution brings communism to Russia.
1929	A worldwide economic depression begins.
1939	World War II begins.
1945	World War II ends.
1969	Humans land on the Moon.
1975	The Vietnam War ends.
1989	The Berlin Wall is torn down as communism crumbles in Eastern Europe.
1991	The Soviet Union breaks into separate states.
2001	Terrorists attack the World Trade Center in New York City and the Pentagon near Washington, D.C.
2004	A tsunami in the Indian Ocean destroys coastlines in Africa, India, and Southeast Asia.
2008	The United States elects its first African American president.

Fast Facts

Official name: Mongolia

Capital: Ulaanbaatar

Official language: Mongolian

Official religion: None

Ulaanbaatar

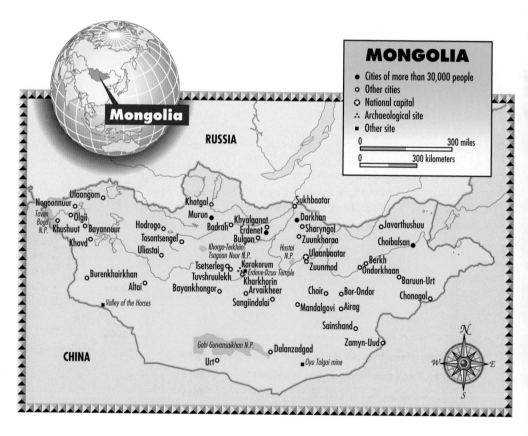

MONGOLIA

- ● Cities of more than 30,000 people
- ○ Other cities
- ⊙ National capital
- ∴ Archaeological site
- ■ Other site

0 — 300 miles

0 — 300 kilometers

RUSSIA

CHINA

Ulaangom
Nogoonnuur
Tavan Bogd N.P.
Olgii
Khushuut
Bayannuur
Khovd
Hodrogo
Tosontsengel
Uliastai
Khatgal
Murun
Badrah
Khyalganat
Erdenet
Bulgan
Khorgo-Terkhiin Tsagaan Nuur N.P.
Sukhbaatar
Darkhan
Sharyngol
Zuunkharaa
Hustai N.P.
Ulaanbaatar
Javarthushuu
Choibalsan
Berkh
Ondorkhaan
Baruun-Urt
Burenkhairkhan
Altai
Tsetserleg
Tuvshruulekh
Karakorum
Erdene-Dzuu Temple
Kharkhorin
Zuunmod
Bayankhongor
Arvaikheer
Choir
Bor-Ondor
Chonogol
Sangiindalai
Mandalgovi
Airag
Valley of the Horses
Sainshand
Gobi Gurvansaikhan N.P.
Dalanzadgad
Zamyn-Uud
Urt
Oyu Tolgoi mine

N
W E
S

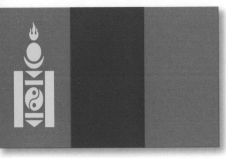
National flag

National anthem: "Mongol ulsyn töriin duulal" (National Anthem of Mongolia)

Type of government: Parliamentary democracy

Head of state: President

Head of government: Prime minister

Area of country: 603,908 square miles (1,564,115 sq km)

Latitude and longitude of Ulaanbaatar: 47.9286° N 106.9124° E

Bordering countries: Russia to the north and China to the south, east, and west

Highest elevation: Mount Huiten, 14,350 feet (4,374 m) above sea level

Lowest elevation: Hoh Lake, 1,873 feet (570 m) above sea level

Deepest lake: Hovsgol Lake, 860 feet (262 m)

Longest river: Orkhon, about 700 miles (1,130 km) long

Average high temperature: In Ulaanbaatar, 4°F (−16°C) in January, 76°F (25°C) in July

Average low temperature: In Ulaanbaatar, −15°F (−26°C) in January, 55°F (13°C) in July

Average annual precipitation: In Ulaanbaatar, 11 inches (28 cm)

Altai Mountains

Erdene-Dzuu Temple

Currency

National population (2012 est.): 2,796,000

Population of major cities (2013 est.):

Ulaanbaatar	1,226,991
Erdenet	83,379
Darkhan	74,738
Choibalsan	38,537
Murun	35,789

Landmarks:
- ▶ *Erdene-Dzuu Temple*, Kharkhorin
- ▶ *Flaming Cliffs*, Gobi Desert
- ▶ *Khorgo-Terkhiin Tsagaan Nuur National Park*
- ▶ *Hovsgol Lake*
- ▶ *Zanabazar Museum of Fine Arts*, Ulaanbaatar

Economy: Mongolia's greatest source of income is mining. Both China and Russia have established highly productive mines that extract and export copper, gold, coal, uranium, tin, and tungsten. Raising livestock is a major part of the economy, as is the growing tourism industry.

Currency: Mongolian tugrik. In 2015, US$1.00 equaled 1,993 tugriks.

System of weights and measures: Metric system

Literacy rate (2015): 98%

Schoolchildren

Byambasuren Davaa

Mongolian words and phrases:

Sain baina uu?	Hello.
Bayartai.	Good-bye.
Ta sain suuj baina uu?	How are you?
Bi sain. Ta sain uu?	I am fine. How are you?
Mash ikh bayarlalaa.	Thank you very much.
Zugeer zugeer.	You're welcome.

Prominent Mongolians:

Byambasuren Davaa   (1971–)
Filmmaker

Chinggis Khan   (1162–1227)
Ruler who established the Mongol Empire

Kublai Khan   (1215–1294)
Ruler over Mongolia and China

Mandukhai Khatun   (1449–1510)
Empress

Sonam Gyatso   (1543–1588)
Dalai Lama

Zanabazar   (1635–1723)
Artist, sculptor, architect, and lama

To Find Out More

Books

▶ Bridges, Shirin Yim. *Sorghaghtani of Mongolia.* Foster City, CA: Goosebottom Books, 2010.

▶ Helget, Nicole. *Mongols.* Mankato, MN: Creative Education, 2013.

▶ Montgomery, Sy. *Saving the Ghost of the Mountain.* Boston: Houghton Mifflin Books for Children, 2009.

Video

▶ Davaa, Byambasuren. *Cave of the Yellow Dog.* New York: Palisades Tartan, 2007.
A nomad girl on the steppe finds a puppy, who becomes her best friend.

▶ *Globe Trekker: Mongolia.* Los Angeles: Pilot Productions, 2010.
A journey through Mongolia's spectacular landscape.

▶ Visit this Scholastic Web site for more information on Mongolia:
www.factsfornow.scholastic.com
Enter the keyword Mongolia

Index

Page numbers in *italics* indicate illustrations.

Internet, 78
Islamic religion, 48, 82, 91, 99, *99*

J

judicial branch of government, 63, 64–65

K

Kashmir goats, 71–72, *71*
Kazakh language, 82, 85
Kazakh people, 80, 82, 99, 124
Khalkha dialact, 81
Khalkha people, 81, 82
Khamnigan people, 84
Khangai Mountains, 16, 24
khasha (camps), 12
Khentii range, 23
Kherlen River, 23
kheviin boov ("shoe sole cake"), 120
Khitan Khanate, 45, *45*
Khorgo-Terkhiin Tsagaan Nuur
   National Park, 38
Khotogoid people, 82
Khoton people, 82, 84
Kublai Khan, 49–51, *51*, 97, 133
Kugultinov, David, 113, *113*

L

lamas (Buddhist holy men). *See also*
   Buddhism.
   architecture and, 108
   Bogd Khan as, 57
   Bogd Khan Uul monastery, 39, *39*
   conversions by, 98–99
   Erdene-Dzuu temple complex, 100,
      100
   Maidar Ergekh holiday, 125–126,
      126
   Murun and, 27
   Phagpa as, 97
   Sakya Pandita, 98
   Soviet Union and, 101

thangka art, 107, *107*
   Zanabazar as, 109
languages, 50, 81, 82, 84, 85–87, *87*
larch trees, *28*
legislative branch of government, 62,
   62, 63–64, *64*, 84
Ligden, Oeled Chahar, 113
literature, 112–113, *113*
livestock. *See also* agriculture; animal
   life.
   camels, 8, 9–10, 12, 35, 86
   cows, 43, 71
   "five snouts," 43, 71
   goats, 9, *25*, 43, 71–72, *71*
   Gobi Desert, 9, *25*
   horses, *19*, 35, *35*, 43, 71, 122–123,
      122, 125
   Kashmir goats, 71–72, *71*
   nomads and, 42–43, 69–70
   pastureland, 9, 70
   population, 71
   reindeer, 83, *83*
   sheep, 9, *11*, *25*, 43, 71
   steppe, 9, *19*, *19*
   weddings and, 117
   zud (weather event) and, 11–12,
      26

M

Maidar (Buddha of the Future),
   125–126
Maidar Ergekh holiday, 125–126, *126*
Mandukhai Khatun, 53, *53*, 133
mantras, 98
manufacturing, 73–74, *75*, 89
maps. *See also* historical maps.
   political, *10*
   population density, *89*
   resources, *72*
   topographical, *20*
   Ulaanbaatar, *67*
marine life, 37, *37*

marmots, 34
marriage, 117, *117*
marshes, 32
military, 47, *47*, 49, 57, 62
Ming dynasty, 39, 52, 53
mining, 12, 27, 72–73, *73*, 74, 116
Modu Chanyu, 44
monasteries. *See also* Buddhism.
   Bogd Khan and, 57
   Bogd Khan Uul monastery, 39, *39*
   construction of, 98, 99, 101, 108,
      112
   Erdene-Dzuu temple complex, 100,
      100
   monks at, *95*
   Murun as, 27
   Soviet Union and, 89, 100, 101,
      110
   Ulaanbaatar as, 67
Mongol Derby, 123
Mongol Empire. *See also* government.
   Altan Khan, 51–52
   archery, 123
   Bogd Khan, 57, *57*
   Chagatai Khan, 50
   Chinggis Khan, 45–48, *46*, *47*, *48*,
      49, 81, 84, 95
   Dayan Khan, 53
   Golden Horde, 48, 50
   Ilkhan Khan, 50
   Khitan Khan, 45
   Kublai Khan, 49–51
   map of, *50*
   National Museum of Mongolia, 67
   Sorghaghtani Beki, 50, *50*
   Uighur Khanate, 44
Mongolian Great Khural, 62, 63–64,
   64, 84
Mongolian language, 85, 86, 87
Mongolian People's Revolutionary
   Party (MPRP), 59

Meet the Author

RUTH BJORKLUND GREW UP IN RURAL NEW ENGLAND where she went hiking, rowing, and sailing. She left New England, traveled, and eventually settled in Seattle, Washington, where she attended the University of Washington. There, she earned a bachelor's degree in comparative literature and a master's degree in library and information science. She has been a children's and young adult librarian and has written many books on a wide range of subjects, including states and countries, Native Americans, health, endangered animals, and contemporary issues such as alternative energy and immigration.

Today, Bjorklund lives on Bainbridge Island, a ferry ride away from Seattle. She enjoys kayaking, sailing, camping, and traveling. In 2006, she traveled to the Gobi Desert and the high country on the border of Mongolia. Staying with the Kazakh and the Uighur people, she slept in gers, rode horses in the mountains and camels in the desert, drank mare's milk tea, and enjoyed the bustle of a Saturday livestock market. She considers it an honor to have been in such a spectacular landscape meeting such creative, hardworking, and gracious people.

Photo Credits

Maps by Mapping Specialists.